The White Cockade

The White Cockade

And Other Jacobite Tales

by

Stuart McHardy

BIRLINN

First published in 2006 by
Birlinn Limited
West Newington House
10 Newington Road
Edinburgh EH9 1QS

www.birlinn.co.uk

ISBN10: 1 84158 441 X
ISBN13: 978 1 84158 441 6

British Library Cataloguing-in-Publication Data
A catalogue record for this book is
available from the British Library

Typeset by Hewer Text UK Ltd, Edinburgh
Printed and bound by Antony Rowe Ltd, Chippenham

This book is dedicated
to storytellers everywhere

Contents

Introduction

In 1822 George IV visited Scotland; he was the first British monarch to do so in over a century. He asked if it was possible to meet any of the men who had fought against his grandfather. An old Knoydart man called Raonull Mor a' Chrolen was amongst those brought to meet the sovereign. After some pleasantries, the king said, 'Well, I suppose you must have often regretted your role in that sad affair many times since then.'

The reply was not slow in coming, 'Your Majesty, I regret nothing of the kind.'

The king's attendants were shocked, and George himself was a bit taken aback at such bluntness. No one was quite sure what would happen next; this grizzled old veteran had just insulted the king! The situation however was softened a bit when Old Raonull added, 'What I did then for the Prince, I would have done as heartily for Your Majesty if you had been in the Prince's place.'

From Sir Walter Scott onwards much has been written about the Jacobite cause and its Romantic figurehead Prince Charles Edward Stewart. However, it is sometimes forgotten that the Jacobites, and Prince Charlie himself, were still actively trying to regain the British throne as late as the 1760s. In 1759 a major invasion of Britain was only prevented by the British naval victory over the French at Quiberon Bay. Thirty thousand troops, a considerable number of them under Prince Charles's command, were in the Channel ports ready to embark. There had also been a short invasion of Ireland a couple of years earlier, and various European states, Prussia and Sweden in particular, had given consideration to helping the Jacobites invade. As late as 1779, proposals were still being made for invasion, showing that the Jacobite threat was sustained for much longer than is generally acknowledged by British historians. This meant the Jacobite cause continued to have meaning in people's hearts and minds in Scotland, where it had always been linked to the widespread resentment caused by the Act of Union of 1707, and is perhaps why Robert Burns, who was a political Radical, wrote so many pro-Jacobite songs. Such an apparent contradiction might well have had a lot to do with the fact that Bonnie Prince himself, after renouncing Catholicism and becoming a Protestant, put forward a political programme in the 1750s that was remarkably forward thinking. It included plans for reform of the notoriously corrupt British electoral process and was in favour of religious and civil liberties. A far cry indeed from the Divine Right of Kings!

The brutal treatment that Cumberland's troops handed out to the Scottish population, not only in the Highlands, also fed into continuing support for the Jacobite cause in Scotland. There is no doubt that a strong streak of Jacobitism continued in Scotland long after any possibility of the restoration of the Stewarts had passed. Some commentators have seen this as little more than a Romantic attachment to an essentially nostalgic view of the past – more Walter Scott than Rabbie Burns. However, the reality of ongoing guerrilla fighting in the 1750s, a further attempt at invasion at the close of that decade and the continuing paranoia of the British Government about rebellion in Scotland, lasting into the 1790s, all suggest something a bit more considered, and deep-rooted. The widespread brutality of the British Army, led by the Duke of Cumberland, lasting into the 1750s as a deliberate Government policy, is perhaps why so many different areas of

Scotland have retained stories about Prince Charlie and why, despite a history of ineptitude and factionalism amongst the Jacobite plotters themselves, their cause still holds a cherished place in the Scottish psyche.

Perhaps it has something to do with the fact that British historians have rarely seen any need to treat Scotland as anything more than a northern district of the island of Britain, while many Scots remember that we were a country before England was, even if we do not all want to revert to our separate existence. From the historical perspective much remains to be done before we fully understand and come to terms with the Jacobite period of our history, and, for all its tragedy, we should remember that at the time of Culloden, and for a long time afterwards, no one thought that the Jacobites were finished. Indeed, recent research showing that the Battle of Culloden was a much closer-run thing than has been understood till now reflects the reality of a situation that was not clear-cut. True, there was a conflict between modern mercantile British society and the ancient, essentially tribal system of the Gaelic-speaking warrior clans. However, the Jacobites had support throughout Scotland and also in England, making the Jacobite rebellions in the seventeenth and eighteenth centuries an ongoing civil war rather than a clash of civilisations. That the Scots resented British rule, as some still do, is reflected in the hold that the Jacobites still have in Scotland. A hold that is reflected in the diversity of the stories presented here.

BATTLE TALES

The Battle of Killiecrankie

⇒•◊•⇐

> I fought on land, I fought on sea
> At hame I fought ma auntie-o
> But I met the Devil an Dundee
> On the Braes o Killiecrankie-o.

This verse from the famous Scots song 'Killiecrankie' sums up the feelings of a soldier on the Government side at the fateful battle of 27 June 1689. The outcome of this battle, if it had been but slightly different, might well have altered the subsequent history not just of Scotland but of the whole British Isles. When the English parliament deposed King James VII in 1688 and replaced him with William of Orange, the Jacobite cause came into being. One of the most prominent of the early Jacobites was John Graham of Claverhouse, Viscount Dundee. An experienced and able soldier, Claverhouse reminded many of an earlier protagonist of the Stewarts, the Marquis of Montrose, also a Graham and a kinsman, who had fought for King Charles II in the 1640s and 50s. John Graham was a bit of a Romantic and modelled himself on Montrose, though he hoped to escape the fate of his kinsman. Montrose had been executed and, in time-honoured fashion, parts of his body had been sent around the country to be displayed on spikes at the gates of major towns. In his youth, Claverhouse saw the dessicated leg of Montrose displayed at Perth, and this is likely to have strengthened his loyalty to the Stewarts. He has come down in tradition and history as one of the great Scottish heroes for one particular reason: he gave his life to win the Battle of Killiecrankie.

By the time William of Orange was installed as king in 1689, Claverhouse was already an experienced soldier, having served in the French army in the 1760s. Ironically, one of his companions at that time was Hugh Mackay, who ended up commanding the Government forces at Killiecrankie! When the Lords of Convention met in Scotland to accept William as king, Claverhouse stormed out, and the song 'Up wi the Bonnets o Bonnie Dundee' quotes him as saying 'Ere the king's crown go down/ There are crowns to be broke.' At this point the Treaty of Union had not yet been foisted on the Scottish people, and, although the crowns of Scotland and England were conjoined, the two countries were still separate entities. Claverhouse was, of course, loyal to King James VII, who had been deposed in England, and when the Convention voted to accept William he knew what he had to do. He left Edinburgh and headed north to raise an army, which was composed almost exclusively of warriors from the Highland clans and Irish Catholics. On 26th July this Highland force met a British Government force under General Mackay at Killiecrankie, a narrow pass through the mountains north of Pitlochry.

The two armies were apparently mismatched: Mackay had four thousand trained soldiers, while Claverhouse had half that number of Highlanders, who were in no way similar to the disciplined troops of the Government. The Highlanders were, however, on home ground, and the outcome of this battle between a force of armed clansmen led by a charismatic figure and the disciplined and more mundane army troops provided a romantic template for Jacobite song and story for the next century.

Claverhouse's immediate aim as he approached the Pass of Killiecrankie from the north was to get through the pass and head on to Perth. This would allow him to consolidate his hold on Scotland north of the Tay and build up his power base from there. Mackay, of course, had the explicit task of stopping this from happening. On the day of the battle Mackay managed to get through the Pass of Killiecrankie itself but found that Graham had taken command of much of the high ground just north of the pass. Throughout the day gunfire was exchanged between the two forces, but Dundee had no intention of letting his Highland and Irish troops charge on the enemy with the sun shining in their faces. So it was that it was late in the day before he used the most formidable weapon he had – the Highland charge. This was a brutal and effective form of hand-to-hand combat, and for centuries it had carried all before it. The Highlanders divested themselves of everything but their shirts and weapons and charged down a slope against their enemies. Those who had guns fired them, then dropped them in favour of a technique that had been honed over centuries of use. In the right hand they carried a broad-bladed, double-edged sword, usually with a basket hilt. The left forearm was threaded through two leather loops on the back of a targe – the Highland leather and wood shield which had an iron or steel spike, up to a foot long, in its centre. The left hand held that ubiquitous Highland weapon/tool the dirk, triangular-bladed, razor sharp and also up to a foot in length. Aided by the momentum of the charge, the targe was used to deflect swords, muskets with bayonets, pikes or any other weapon brandished by the man directly in front, while the right hand swept the sword at the man to the right. Once the man in front's weapon was deflected, if the spike of the targe had not already injured him, the dirk was used to stab him. The success of this tactic relied on several factors: the skill of the men with their weapons, their ability to run downhill over rough ground at full speed and, most importantly, the presence of a slope to run down. It was a tactic designed for, and perfected in, the glens of the Scottish mountains, and, as was shown all too well in the later battle of Culloden, it was of less effect on flat ground against firearms. However, it also had the further advantage of being terrifying, a psychological effect that played havoc with enemy resolve, even that of the battle-hardened Lowland troops of General Mackay at Killiecrankie.

The traditional behaviour of the Highland warrior manifested itself in other ways that day. Ewen Cameron of Lochiel was leading his own clansmen and was shadowed by the son of his foster-brother. Fostering was the system by which sons of leading families were brought up in the households of other kinsmen. This meant that, in addition to any brothers of their own, they had the added bonus of foster-brothers, a considerable advantage for those who were destined to become chiefs. In effect, the young chief was being given a second family and it was said that the loyalty of foster-brothers was unsurpassable. Lochiel was in the thick of the battle and realised that his faithful companion was no longer by his side. In a brief break in the hand-to-hand fighting he turned to look around. There, a few yards behind him, lay his loyal kinsman, on his back with an arrow sticking out of his chest. Lochiel ran back to where he lay, knelt down and lifted his head gently.

'Ochone, ochone,' he said, 'they have shot you my good friend.'

'Ach, well,' gasped the dying man, 'I saw that one of those damned Government men, a Highlander like ourselves, had nocked his arrow and had you in his sights. I could not let him shoot you Locheil, now could I?'

And, saying that, he gave a last gasp and died in the arms of his chief. If he had been furious in battle till then, Locheil was now like a berserker of old and he and his Cameron kin swept through the Government forces like a wind of death. It was a costly attack

8

though, for they lost over a hundred men in that fierce battle. Before the battle itself started, Claverhouse had asked Lochiel who should have the victory. Like many Highlanders, Lochiel had the gift, or, more truly, the curse, of the second sight – the ability to discern the future. His reply was simple: 'He who draws the first blood, shall win the day.'

Now, with the Jacobite army being almost completely formed of Highlanders, who had a great respect for the second sight and those who had the gift of it, Lochiel's words ran through the ranks like wildfire. When his words reached the contingent from the Grant clan, Grant of Glenmoriston knew what to do.

'Where's Iain Beg?' he cried to his men.

Iain Beg MacRae, famed among his kin for his skill with the gun, was called for and came running to where Glenmoriston stood.

'Here I am,' he said, 'what would you have me do?'

Glenmoriston pointed towards the enemy rank. There, riding along the enemy lines, was an officer on a white horse.

'Well, Euan, does that white horse not make its rider a good target?' he asked with a grim smile. 'Aye, so it does,' replied the other. And, lifting his gun to his shoulder, he sighted along the barrel. All the Grants held their breath. He fired. His aim was good. The rider in the distance threw up his arms, his horse reared and he fell to the earth, still. All along the Highland line the cheers rang out. The first blood was theirs, and they now had no doubt that victory would follow. Who could argue with fate? A nearby well, *Fuaran u trupar*, the Trooper's Well, was renamed later to show where the horseman fell. Soon the battle was being fiercely fought, hand-to-hand, over a considerable area. One of Mackay's officers in the pass itself, Brigadier-General Balfour, a Lowland Scot, saw his men fall around him under the onslaught of the Highland troops. One after another the men with him fell, till at last he was on his own, forced back against a tree fending off two assailants with his sword. One of these was Alastair Ban Stewart. As the general bravely defended himself against his assailants, Alastair Ban's son came up. Seeing the soldier putting up such a good fight against two enemies, he called out in Gaelic. 'Shame, shame on you father, give the brave man his life.'

Alastair Ban and his companion stepped back, turned and looked at the young man as Balfour took the opportunity to suck in great breaths of air.

Coming closer, the younger Stewart complimented the officer in English on his skill as a swordsman. Like all Highland lads, he had been brought up with the notion of *cothrom na Feinne*, the fair play of Finn McCoul, and Highland tradition had long focused on fighting one to one. In the heat of battle, however, such niceties were easily forgotten. He had merely been trying to remind his father of the right way of doing things when he called out. The reaction of the Lowlander to this intrusion was not at all what he had expected.

'To hell with you, you Highland dog,' cried Balfour, who was fired up by the battle conditions as much as his opponents were, and he lunged at the young Highlander.

At this, young Stewart moved nimbly to one side and swung his great claymore down on Balfour's collar bone, slicing through his body as far as his waist.

'Now there was a man who did not know when he was well off,' his father said to him before they headed off back to the battle. Not far from the scene of the battle is a large flat stone known as the Balfour Stone, where it has been said the unfortunate Brigadier-General was buried afterwards.

A Government sentry had been stationed near the south end of the pass, and the first he knew of the outcome of the battle was when he saw a group of Highlanders rushing towards him. He immediately took to his heels and ran for the River Garry.

His pursuers were catching up, and he was sure that they had him as he was running towards a rock jutting out over the river below; in fact one of them had scratched his shoulder with his sword. In his desperation to escape, the trooper leapt out from the rock over the river. As he fell on the other side, he reached out and grabbed a bush to stop himself falling back. Behind him the Highlanders had stopped, and there are those who say that one of them tried to shoot the fleeing soldier. His companions stopped him, reckoning that his bravery in leaping out over the river entitled the soldier to escape; *cothrom na Feinne* still mattered. From then on the local people referred to this spot as the Soldier's Leap.

The Government troops were routed, and many of them were killed on the battlefield, or in the following pursuit, although about five hundred of them were taken prisoner.

The battle was going well for the Jacobites when Claverhouse stood up in his stirrups to signal his horsemen to charge the Government troops of Leven's regiment, who were still standing firm. As he lifted himself up a bullet entered under his raised arm and he was thrown from his horse. He fell to the ground, mortally wounded, and, even as his men triumphed over their enemies, he breathed his last on the heather. With the loss of such a talented and charismatic leader the Jacobite cause itself suffered a terrible blow. A few days later the Highland army was driven back from a fire-fight at the town of Dunkeld, fifteen or so miles south of Killiecrankie, and the rebellion was effectively over. Again a Highland army dispersed like smoke into the hills and glens. Yet even victory was not enough for some of Claverhouse's enemies, and the story was soon going the rounds that he had, in fact, been killed by one of his own men, who wanted to rid the country of Popery and the Stewarts who supported it! Some incurable Romantics also like to believe that beneath his iron breastplate Graham was wearing Knights Templar uniform! Stories gather round heroes, and, in defeating a larger Government force only to die in the heather, Claverhouse left a legend that has inspired many a story and song since.

Disaster at Preston

⇒•◆•⇐

In the history of the Jacobite rebellions in Britain there have been some notable victories, but there have also been more than a few absolute disasters. In the 1715 Rising the indecisive leadership of John Erskine, the Earl of Mar, known as Bobbing John for his habit of changing sides – he had been the British Government's chief representative in Scotland – led directly to the shambles of the Battle of Sherrifmuir. However, he was not the only ditherer and was matched by another Jacobite Leader, Thomas Forster, the Earl of Derwentwater and Member of Parliament for Northumberland. Like many of the Jacobites in Scotland and England, Forster was an Episcopalian, and he ended up in command of a combined Scottish and English force in the Borders at the end of September. The Scottish contingent consisted of both Lowlanders from Lothian and a detachment of over a thousand Highlanders, under the command of Mackintosh of Borlum, who had been sent south by Mar to increase the effectiveness of what was a second, if small, Jacobite army. Mar stayed at Perth with the rest of the troops, doing nothing. From the very beginning there was disagreement between the Scots and English. While the Scots wanted to secure the Borders, Forster and his compatriots insisted on heading south to raise further support for the rebellion. Forster, in particular, no doubt inspired by the fact that many northern English cities had seen riots when George I was installed on the throne after the death of Queen Anne, was certain that

13

great numbers of Episcopalians would flock to the cause as they passed down through Lancashire towards his intended target, Liverpool. Having been given command, as the only non-Catholic amongst the leadership, in the hope that English Episcopalians would rally to the cause, he eventually had his way, although not before creating a considerable amount of ill feeling amongst the Scots and destroying the morale of his command.

As the combined force headed south they were being shadowed by local militia groups, who had been mobilised by magistrates in the area on Government instructions. They did not have enough force to attack the Jacobites, but their presence no doubt helped to prevent Jacobite recruitment. On 7 November, Forster and the Jacobites marched into Lancaster in great style, their colours flying and swords drawn, to the sound of bagpipes and drums. They made a tremendous spectacle, still remembered fondly in Lancaster, and the Old Pretender was proclaimed King James III of England at the town cross. They were welcomed by a considerable number of local notables, and five local gentlemen publicly joined the force. This was a great deal less than Forster had been hoping for, but while they occupied the town they managed to obtain half-a-dozen small cannon from a ship moored in the harbour. Two days later, after this pleasant diversion, they marched out of the town towards Preston. Heading south, Forster got reports that a large force was in his path, as many as ten thousand men. In fact, this was a force of local people, forced out by the Bishop of Carlisle and Lord Lonsdale, most of whom were armed with no more than agricultural tools. On seeing the Highlanders approach, most of them turned and ran; the rest were simply swept out of the way.

The upshot of this skirmish was that the Jacobites simply confiscated what little decent weaponry, horses and stores this ragged mob had with them and pressed on south. On 9 November the force marched into Preston, a thriving town with many substantial houses and quite a few narrow alleys separating the blocks of houses. While the troops were being billeted throughout the town, some more gentlemen came forward to offer their services to the Jacobite cause. Just as had happened in Lancaster, they were all Catholics. The Episcopalians and High Tory Anglicans Forster was hoping would join up kept themselves to themselves. The Catholics were a persecuted minority and had reason to rise, but, without the support of a much broader base in the population, the whole prospect of victory in England was clearly fading. The fact that two companies of dragoons had left Preston without putting up a fight gave little comfort: it was clearly a tactical decision. There was no doubt that Forster would soon be hearing of larger numbers of Government troops. The situation was grim, and it seems that the leader responded by retiring to his bed. However, he still had a considerable number of troops, nearly two thousand, including Borlum's Highlanders, who were eager to get to grips with the enemy.

They soon had their wish, for on 12 November scouts brought word that General Wills was approaching from the south with a considerable force. It was decided to put up a fight in Preston itself, and soon trenches were being dug and barricades erected in the main streets. All at once, the situation seemed to be improving. Action is always preferable to waiting, and the town provided a good defensive position. Troops were appointed to their positions and reserves were deployed in the centre of the town, ready to support any part of the defences as needed.

When the Government troops mounted their first assault they suffered heavy fire from the muskets of Borlum's Highlanders, who were shooting from windows, while the cannon appropriated in Lancaster, directed by a sailor from the ship that had provided them, poured vicious and deadly grape-shot into the advancing attackers. Despite the fact that this sailor had celebrated joining the Jacobite cause by getting drunk every day since, the cannons had a deadly effect, and by the time the Hanoverian forces reached the first barricades on Church Street their numbers were sorely depleted. Their first attack was repulsed with severe losses, and the Jacobites cheered as they retreated. This was what so many of them had been waiting for, and their first engagement with the enemy forces appeared to have gone very well.

The Government army's next attack was a bit more successful than the first. Troops were sent to try and set fire to the houses and other buildings to the east of the Church Street barricades. The Hanoverians managed to do this, but the wind veered and the smoke under which they had hoped to mount another attack was blown back in their faces. Some of them, though, did manage to get into the wynds and alleys of the south end of the town, where a group of over a hundred men gathered under the command of a captain. They stormed Patten House, which provided a commanding position over the barricades at the head of Church Street. This was a serious problem. If they could fire down on the Jacobites at the barricades it would make it much easier for their comrades to mount a successful assault on them and get into the town itself.

Fighting was vicious by now, and the Highlanders mounted a direct assault on this Government force, attacking via a back lane just as night fell. Yet again the Highland forces proved their effectiveness at close quarters, and the soldiers were driven back, leaving nearly a hundred and fifty dead behind them. By now, though, the policy of firing buildings was taking effect and the night sky flared with flames. General Wills's men now had a toehold in the town, and, as most of them were well-trained and battle-hardened, the battle raged fiercely. The order then came for the Government troops to put lighted candles in the houses they had captured so their officers could see what progress was being made. The canny Jacobites soon noticed this, and candles began appearing in so many windows that the intention of the Hanoverian forces was totally thwarted. Soon after this the fighting died back to sporadic outbursts of gunfire as the men on both sides lay down where they were and tried to snatch whatever sleep was possible before dawn and the inevitable resurgence of hostilities. By this time, Thomas Forster, instead of inspecting the defences and thus instilling a bit of morale in his force, had gone to his bed.

Come the morning, though, things had changed. Overnight, a further contingent of Government troops had arrived from Newcastle under the command of General Carpenter, over two and half thousand of them, and this gave Wills enough men to totally surround Preston. The choices for the Jacobites were now stark. They had made no preparations for a long siege – Forster's optimistic assessment of the situation had led to them planning to be in Preston for no more than couple of days – and there was no way of holding out for any protracted period. They would have to fight their way out through the Government troops or surrender where they were. It was that simple. To the Mackintosh clansmen who had come down from Scotland there was no question. They had done alright against these trained soldiers of the regular army up to this point and wanted only to be organised for a rush on the troops to the north of the city. Borlum, along with the Earl of Wintoun, agreed with this position. They had already inflicted major casualties on their enemy, morale among their troops was high and they were still in command of their strongest positions, which would allow them some room for manoeuvre. The answer was simple: to lay plans accordingly and get ready to fight their way out! Their commander, however, did not agree.

Forster, having already shown himself as almost incapable of decisive action, now acted decisively, but disastrously. One of his companions from the start, Oxburgh, who had been given the rank of general during the fiasco of the southern campaign, was sent out, unknown to the Scots contingent, under a flag of truce to General Wills. His orders were simple: get whatever terms you can and we will surrender! Wills at first had no intention of dealing with any 'damned rebel' but was prevailed upon by Scottish officers in his regiment to at least listen to Oxburgh. He heard him out then gave his terms.

'I will spare your lives if you all surrender. You have one hour then I will send in my men with orders for no quarter,' he said in a harsh voice.

When Oxburgh returned with the offer Forster caved in immediately. The news spread like wildfire. The Scots, and in particular the clan Mackintosh, were outraged. They well knew that they would be tried as rebels and that their lives would probably be forfeit. One of the officers, Captain Dalzell, then went to General Wills to try and get specific terms for the Highlanders. He was spurned out of hand. Both Borlum and Wintoun, having sworn to follow Forster's orders, seemed to think, reluctantly or not, that they had to accept. Not all felt the same way. Before anything else transpired, one of the Lowland Scots, Murray, went to Forster's apartments. Bursting in, he levelled his pistol at the supposed general and pulled the trigger. Just at that point, one of Forster's companions, one Patten, intervened and knocked Murray's arm up. Murray was immediately seized by other officers. It is not difficult to imagine the words chosen by Murray as his attempt on Forster's life failed. Like many others, he knew his fate was sealed. And his actions were no different from what was in the hearts of many of the other Scots that day. As for Patten, he turned King's Evidence at Murray's trial and later left his own account of the happenings of 1715, for what they are worth.

The Jacobite army laid down its weapons in Preston on 14 November. On the same day, a couple of hundred miles to the north, another battle was being fought. This was the battle of Sheriffmuir, after which the Earl of Mar made his excuses and left Scotland for the Continent. It was indeed a black day for the Jacobite cause, snatching defeat from the jaws of victory. All the more bitter because the casualties at Preston were seventeen dead for the Jacobites against over two hundred on the Hanoverian side.

And as for the men who surrendered at Preston, betrayed by their leadership, their fate was harsh indeed. Although both Mackintosh and Wintoun managed to escape after they were condemned to death and jailed, the lot of the 'common' soldiers was dreadful. Most of them were locked up in churches in Preston, guarded by troops, but reliant on the locals for food, and not even given blankets or extra clothing as the winter closed in. According to local contemporary accounts, they were forced to tear the linings from the pews to try and make coverings for themselves. Dozens of them died then, either of starvation or brutality, in various English prisons. The majority of the rest were sent off as slaves to the plantations in the West Indies. Mackintosh managed to escape from Newgate and went to France, returning to take part in the further abortive Jacobite Rising in 1719, after which he again escaped to the Continent. However, he could not keep away from his beloved Highlands and returned once more. He was captured in 1727 and spent the rest of his days, till his death in 1745, as a prisoner in Edinburgh Castle.

As for Thomas Forster, the Earl of Derwentwater, his wishy-washy behaviour and rank cowardice in the end did him little harm. He escaped from Newgate in the following April in circumstances that hinted at Government collusion. By then, a suitable postscript to the disaster of Preston and the fiasco of Sheriffmuir had already taken place. James III had landed in Scotland in December, come at last to rally his support in the country of his ancestors, but, as all too often with the Jacobites, it was too little, too late.

Not the Battle of Inverary

⟫◆⟪

There are many examples of rather pathetic leadership skills amongst the Jacobites in 1715, but they were not alone. As it was still the norm in those days for aristocrats to advance to the most senior military ranks with little or no regard for actual tactical or strategic skills, this is hardly very surprising. In October, General Alexander Gordon of Auchintool was sent to the west of Scotland by the Earl of Mar. He marched on Inverary, the chief seat of the Campbells in their Argyll homelands, with a force of four thousand men. The Duke of Argyll's brother, Archibald Campbell, the Earl of Islay, was in charge of the forces loyal to the Hanoverians in the west, and he had fortified the town itself by digging trenches and gathering in nearly two and a half thousand men, including regular troops and Campbell clansmen. Some of his forces were cavalry.

Gordon made his camp a mile or so to the north-east of Inverary. Whether or not he was eager for battle is unclear for it seems that, on the advice of the Jacobite Campbell of Glendaruel, he was hoping to gather a number of new recruits from Argyll and the adjoining areas. Gordon thought that if he could keep Islay and his troops cornered in Inverary the chances of men flocking to join him would be that much greater. Islay, meanwhile, having found out that the Jacobite army was considerably larger than the numbers of troops at his command, was reluctant to sally forth and close with the enemy. So, matters stood at a bit of a standstill for a few days with neither side doing very much at all.

Following Campbell of Glendaruel's advice, Gordon decided to send out a recruiting party. A force of about two hundred men was sent out under the leadership of Campbell of Glenlyon, another of his clan that was siding with the Stewarts. It was thought that a Campbell would have the best chance of attracting new men in the district of Lorn: Campbell country. The Duke of Islay soon got word of what was happening. To counteract this effort he sent out a troop of seven hundred clansmen under the leadership of one of the most experienced soldiers of his clan, Colonel Campbell of Fonab. He set off north to try and intercept Glenlyon. Right enough, he came alongside the Jacobite force near a wee village or clachan at the foot Loch Nell, a few miles east of Oban. When they saw the Hanoverian men approaching, the Jacobite forces drew themselves up in line of battle across the side of small hill. Fonab's men drew up opposite them, and it was immediately clear that the Jacobites were outnumbered at least three to one. As he was mulling over whether to fight or flee, Glenlyon saw a horseman detach from the opposite ranks. Obviously this was to be an attempt at having a parley. Spurring his own horse, he moved forward, recognising as he did so that his opposite number was Fonab.

The old soldier rode up to him and the pair of them stopped midway between the two forces.

'Well then, Glenlyon, are you well?' said Fonab politely.

'I am indeed, Fonab, are you keeping well yourself?' he replied, pleased to see the older man despite the situation.

'Och well, this is a pretty pass we have come to,' Fonab went on, 'and I think it would be great disaster if we were to see Campbell fighting Campbell this day.'

22

'I would agree with that,' relied Glenlyon slowly, 'but what have you in mind?'

At that, Fonab told his younger kinsman what he thought should happen. The two of them sat on horseback between their respective forces then Glenlyon turned and rode back to his men to tell them of what was proposed. Well, not just proposed, but proposed and accepted. In order to avoid the horror of the clansmen fighting their own kin, Fonab suggested that Glenlyon's men should hand over their arms, he could ask no less. For his part, he and his men would convoy them out of Argyll and then release them to return to their own army. Glenlyon, well aware that there were plenty of arms back with the main body of the Jacobite army at Perth, saw the sense in this; he, too, had no wish to see Campbells spilling Campbell blood and so happily accepted the terms. Accordingly, Fonab's men accompanied the Glenlyon's men to the edge of Argyll, where they happily waved farewell to their cousins, who headed back to join the Jacobite army. On hearing of this from Fonab, the Earl of Islay was furious, and he loudly berated the old soldier in front of a group of other officers. It was precisely this sort of behaviour that led many of the Campbells at Inverary to decide that Islay was getting above himself, and there was a consequent outbreak of desertion, amongst both officers and men. The quality of leadership on both sides was clearly no match for the courage, commitment and, in this case, intelligence of the men under their command.

A day or so after the Jacobites had arrived, the Campbells in Inverary were wakened in the night by a great noise of thundering hooves. The immediate suspicion was that the Jacobites were attacking with cavalry, and men quickly formed up around the castle with their arms, ready to repulse the enemy. As they stood ready to fire, the hooves got louder, and suddenly there in front of them was herd of horses. Not one had a saddle, a bridle, or a rider. This was the herd of horses brought by Campbells and MacEacherns from Kintyre to provide Islay with some cavalry. Ever since Roman times, when the local tribe was known as the Epidii, or horse warriors, the Kintyre men had been famous for their skill with horses, the name MacEachern itself meaning son of the horse. In this case, however, they had not looked after their stock well and had left them on a poor bit of grazing close to the town. The horses, dissatisfied with their location, had simply decided to move and look for better grazing! While moving across the river to a better meadow, something spooked them, setting off a stampede. With all the rattling of drums and the shouting of the officers, the horses speeded up and headed off westwards into the night. A report of the time said, 'At last the whole was found only to be a plot among the Kintyre horse to desert not to the enemy, but to their own country; for, 'tis to be supposed, the horses, as well as their owners, were of very loyal principles.' This put an end to Islay's cavalry for the meantime, and once the horses had gone the majority of the men went back to sleep.

Later the very same night, a sergeant was doing the rounds of the sentries at Inverary. The sergeant had spent some hours in a tavern in the town during the evening and was somewhat the worse for wear. As he approached one of the sentries in the dark, the sentry called out, 'Who goes there? State the password.'

The sergeant, due to the amount of drink he had taken, had completely forgotten the password and simply called out. 'It is Sergeant Dougal Campbell . . .'

He got no chance to say any more. The sentry was already nervous because of the earlier incident with the horses, and, not receiving the password, raised his musket and fired at the indistinct figure he could see. The sergeant threw himself to the ground.

Pandemonium broke out. Up in the castle, Islay heard the shot and called at once for the drummer to beat the call to arms. All around the town, men grabbed their muskets and headed for the mustering point on the castle green. The drunken sergeant, sobering up quickly, realised what he had done and, to cover his tracks, gave a great shout, 'The rebels. The rebels are coming!' At once, several other sentries began firing in the general direction of the Jacobite camp.

The main body of the Government force was assembled on the castle green, where the troops were ordered into the trenches adjoining the town and ordered to start firing, platoon by platoon, in the direction of the rebels. No one had any doubt that there was a night attack under way from the north-east. So, volley after volley rang out and orders were shouted by the officers, the majority of whom, it seems, had retired behind the thick walls of Inverary Castle! Up in the Jacobite camp everyone was awakened by the noise, and, looking towards the town, they saw the flashes of the persistent firing. Gordon knew he had not ordered a night attack and took the firing to be a celebration of the arrival of reinforcements for the Hanoverian forces. Deciding that discretion was the better part of valour, he at once put an order round that his men were to march back east as soon as the dawn rose.

Eventually, Islay realised that there was no returning fire, and orders were given to his men to cease firing. Such was the tenseness of the situation that they all stood to arms through the hours of darkness. Come the dawn, it was obvious that there had been no attempted assault by the Jacobites. Only a short while later, word came in that, in fact, the forces of General Gordon were heading back east towards Perth.

The Battle of High Bridge

⟫◆⟪

On 16 August 1745, three days before Prince Charlie raised his standard at Glenfinnan, the Governor of Fort Augustus heard that there was trouble brewing among the people of Moidart and decided to send two companies of troops to Fort William, twenty eight miles south, to reinforce the garrison there. The troops were recent recruits, with no battle experience, and were under the command of a Captain Scott. They had gone some twenty or so miles of their journey and were approaching the High Bridge over the Spean River, which had been erected by General Wade nine years earlier. As they came near to the bridge, they saw a group of armed Highlanders guarding it, with a piper playing a rousing tune. Captain Scott halted his troops at once. He looked and saw that there was great deal of movement, with men coming in and out of the woods beside the bridge. Judging by the noise that they were making, there seemed to be a considerable number of armed clansmen, and he sent two of his men forward to have a better look and to try and figure out just how many men there were at the bridge. The two soldiers were cautiously approaching the bridge, sticking close to the edge of the trees along the road, when, suddenly, they were leapt on by two men. They were thrown to the ground and looked up to see themselves facing the barrels of a pair of pistols. They were hustled along the road to the bridge, an event seen by Captain Scott further back up the road.

Having lost two of his men already, and unwilling to advance into the bottleneck that the road formed as it neared the bridge, Scott decided to retreat for the moment at least. He had no doubt that there was a substantial force of men at the bridge, being unaware that Donald MacDonald of Tirnadris was leading a group of no more than a dozen of his kinsmen. Having been informed that the soldiers were approaching, he had ordered his men to make a lot of noise and to move back and forward between the woods and the bridge to try and convince the soldiers that he had a much larger force. Clearly it had worked. As the troops he headed off, he decided that he and his men should follow them, but not right away or it might become all too obvious that his force was extremely limited. While he waited, he sent one of his kinsmen to the clan chief, Keppoch, who soon joined him with a further twenty MacDonalds. The combined force then headed off after the Government troops, intending to head them off up the road.

Captain Scott realised that something significant was happening. The Highlanders had blatantly kidnapped two of his men, and this was tantamount to a declaration of war. He was effectively in hostile territory and reckoned a return to Fort Augustus the safest course of action. He headed back up Loch Lochy and upon approaching the little village of Laggan Achadrum he saw several groups of Highlanders surrounding it. All of them appeared to be heavily armed. He was not aware that Keppoch and Tirnadris had been fully informed of his troops' movements since they had left Fort Augustus. They had also had news of another Government force heading towards Fort Augustus from Ruthven in Strathspey. Scott decided that, with so many armed men about, he had little chance of making it to either Fort William or Fort Augustus without being forced to fight. Given that the numbers of armed clansmen he thought he had seen greatly outnumbered his own small force, he had to think of something fast. He made a decision to try and take the fortified tower of Invergarry and headed towards it over the narrow strip of land between Loch Lochy and Loch Oich.

It was at this point that Keppoch, Tirnadris and the MacDonalds swept down on them from the hill above. At the same time, a bunch of Kennedys from Glengarry appeared in front of the Redcoats, and the battle was on. The first volley from the Highlanders killed four of the soldiers and Captain Scott fell with a bullet in his shoulder. There was a brief lull and Keppoch stepped forward and called for the Government troops to surrender, or else! The soldiers' position was hopeless, they were out in the open between two enemy forces, and Scott had no option but to surrender. Just as the captain agreed to surrender, a further force of Camerons, under their chief, Lochiel, came marching up from the west. Scott's troops would have had no chance had they not surrendered.

Lochiel imprisoned the troops at Achnacarry and he sent word to Fort William to ask for a doctor to be sent to tend to Captain Scott. When this elicited no response, the captain was taken to the fort by a small group of Camerons and released upon parole. It was later noted that he kept his word and lifted no further hand against the Jacobites.

A day or so later, a further contingent of Government troops, led by Captain Sweetenham, were captured by MacDonald of Lochgarry, and the captured prisoners were paraded before Prince Charles at Glenfinnan. The prince was also presented with the fine white gelding that Captain Scott had been riding at High Bridge. Even if the number of clansmen committing themselves to his cause was a bit disappointing, he must have thought that this was an auspicious start to his campaign.

The news of the captures of two separate contingents of Redcoats sped through the Highlands, and it is generally believed that it helped more than a few waverers to make up their minds and 'come out' for Charlie. Tirnadris, who thus commanded the very first engagement of the rising, later paid a price for his success.

After the Jacobite success at the Battle of Falkirk in January 1746, Tirnadris mistook a group of General Hawley's troops for a patrol of French soldiers commanded by Lord Drummond. He rode up to them and, just as he realised his mistake, he was taken prisoner and was subsequently put on trial at Carlisle. The charge against him was that he had refused to 'give quarter', or in other words spare the lives of defeated enemy soldiers, even when urged to do so by fellow officers. Not a single piece of evidence was given to support this slur on his character. No Jacobite believed that the verdict and subsequent sentence were anything other than the Government taking revenge for him having so successfully opened hostilities in the '45 by capturing Captain Scott and his men. After he was sentenced to be executed, he managed to bribe one of the jailers to loosen his fetters so he could slip them off and try to escape, but he was noticed and the attempt was foiled. He was brutally executed, on 19th October, at Carlisle, by being hung, drawn and quartered.

A siege of his own home

Not all of the supporters of the Stewart cause were Catholics or even Episcopalians; there were also some Presbyterians. There were families who were split over the Jacobite–Hanoverian divide and perhaps none more so then the Murrays, the dukes of Atholl, whose ancestral home was Blair Castle. Lord George Murray, a younger son of the house, was firmly on the side of the Jacobite cause as was his elder brother William, who had lost his title as Duke of Atholl precisely because of his Jacobite sympathies and was known thereafter as the Marquis of Tullibardine. The Government awarded the title to the second brother James, who was as strongly supportive of the Hanoverian cause as his brothers were of the Stewarts. James had fled the castle when Prince Charlie arrived there with a large force of men in August 1745, where he had been effusively greeted by Lady Charlotte Lude, a cousin of the Murrays. On the retreat from England the following year, the Jacobites had neglected to man Blair Castle as they progressed north, and it was soon occupied by a contingent of Government troops under the command of Colonel Sir Andrew Agnew.

With the majority of the Jacobite army now at Inverness, it was thought necessary to take Blair Castle to try to prevent Government troops having a free march north to the Drumochter Pass and on through Strathspey towards Inverness. The castle sits just to the north of the narrow defile of the Pass of Killiecrankie and thus was of considerable strategic importance. So Lord George Murray marched south with his Atholl Brigade, made up of the Menzies and Robertson regiments as well as some Stewarts. Coming down through Badenoch, they were joined by a force of MacPhersons led by their chief, Cluny MacPherson, making the numbers up to around a thousand men. As the Jacobite force came south they overpowered a series of Government outposts with hardly a shot fired and no casualties suffered.

George Murray outflanked the castle and secured the Pass of Killiecrankie, then turned his attention to the castle itself. He set up his headquarters in McGlashan's Inn, in the nearby village of Blair Atholl. He decided to give Agnew a chance to surrender but was aware, like every one else in the Jacobite camp, of Agnew's reputation. Agnew was a fierce and ruthless character and was likely to shoot any messenger who approached the castle, even one carrying a flag of truce. No one among the troops, no grizzled veteran or headstrong youth eager to make a name for himself, was in a hurry to volunteer for the job of taking the message. It seemed a death warrant. Yet somebody had to go. Overhearing the officers discussing the matter, a serving maid at MacGlashan's stepped forward. Her name was Molly Robertson, and she was a rather attractive and eminently sensible lass. Boldly she addressed Murray, 'Ach, I know a lot o the young officers up at the castle, they come in here regularly. I am sure that I could tak a message for ye sirs, and that I would come to nae harm.'

Murray and his officers were a bit taken aback by this confident young woman, but, as soon as they gave the matter thought, all there realised this was the answer to their problem,

'Well, Molly, thank you very much,' said Murrray after a few moments. 'We will be greatly obliged to you if you will take our message to Agnew and his men.'

31

He then wrote a message on a piece of paper, folded it and gave it to the young lass with a sweeping bow.

Molly left the inn and set off for the castle, less than a mile north of the village. Coming close, she waved the paper Lord George had written on and called out that she had a message for Colonel Agnew. She had, of course, been seen from a good way off, and one of the officers called back, 'What message do you have, Molly, and from whom?'

'It is frae Lord George, Willie,' she replied. 'He says that if you surrender you will all be well treated, and I think you would dae weel to tak up his offer, he has a lot o men with him and some o them hae cannons.'

Her words set the watching officers laughing. Them surrender, not likely. One of them shouted down to the lass. 'Don't you worry, Molly, we have nothing to worry about in here. That rabble can do us no harm, and if they come we'll soon drive them off.'

'Weel that is as may be,' she called back, 'but I hae this message here frae Lord George an somebody should come down an get it.'

After a while, one of the officers, a lieutenant, did come out of the castle, and he took the piece of paper from her and promised to take it to Sir Andrew. This he did, and the reaction was perfectly in character for Colonel Agnew. The old soldier ranted and cursed at the sheer effrontery of this Highland rabble and threw the lieutenant out of his room telling him to take the paper back to the messenger, cursing at Lord George and shouting that any further messengers were to be shot on sight, male or female. Molly heard his ranting and, as soon as she had the paper again, ran off at some speed back to the inn in the village. She had no intention of hanging about in case the colonel decided to have her shot for aiding the rebels!

At the inn, she told the Jacobites what had happened, and they too burst out laughing. They were every bit as confident of victory as the ill-tempered colonel. The following morning the siege began. The Jacobites took up their position behind a dyke about three hundred yards from the castle and opened fire with their cannon. These, however, were small field pieces firing four-pound cannonballs and were unlikely to do much damage to the seven-foot-thick stone walls of Blair Castle. When the bombardment began Agnew was astonished. 'Whit's this?' he said. 'Is the loon clean daft, tryin tae knock doun his ain brither's hoose?'

Realising that his cannon could have little effect on the walls, Murray changed his tactics. He had the local smith set up braziers in the nearby St Bride's churchyard to heat the cannon balls till they were red-hot. They were then fired at the roof of the castle, the intention being to set fire to the roof and thus drive the defenders out. Agnew's men, however, were up to the task of putting out any fires that started on the roof. As water was in short supply, the wily colonel had set up barrels of urine at strategic spots, and this was used to dowse the fires that were started. Small-arms fire was exchanged daily, but with one side well entrenched and the other behind seven-foot-thick walls there was little effect from this activity and no one was hurt. In fact, though their supplies were beginning to run a bit short, the men in the castle were a bit bored. They were safe as long as they didn't make easy targets of themselves, and there was really no way the Jacobites could do anything without much heavier artillery. A couple of them found time hanging so heavy on their hands that they decided to have a wee joke.

They mocked up a dummy of Colonel Agnew pointing a spyglass in the enemy's direction and placed it at a prominent window. It was soon the object of increased firing from the Jacobite positions until, that is, Agnew demanded to know what was going on, at which point the effigy was quickly removed and hidden. The lieutenant removing the dummy was the only one of the defenders who was ever really in any danger, but such was the quality of the Jacobite small-arms fire that he was untouched.

The idea of setting fire to his ancestral home preyed on Lord George's mind, and, after a few days of unsuccessful cannonades, he wrote to his brother Tullibardine explaining that he might be forced to demolish the castle, obviously hoping he would intercede. Just how Lord George thought he could achieve this demolition is unclear since the castle's situation on an outcrop of rock made it impossible to mine underneath the walls, a standard siege tactic of the times. In any case, Tullibardine's reply was along the lines of, 'do what you must, but just try to save some of the family portraits!'

By the beginning of April there was no sign of the troops in the castle giving up. They had clearly laid in enough food, even if it was plain fare, to last them for months. Up in Inverness, the prince decided that enough was enough and sent word for Lord George to come back and join the main army. The effort they had spent in trying to capture the castle was not worth it, particularly as they already had control of the Pass of Killiecrankie. So it was that one morning the officers in the castle awoke to find the fields outside Blair Castle deserted.

Well, deserted apart from one figure. There was Molly come back again to tell them that the Jacobites had all gone off in the night and they were welcome to come and have a glass or two in the inn. A typical old soldier, Agnew sent out a heavily armed patrol composed of veteran soldiers to check out how the land lay before the troops were allowed to take Molly up on her offer.

The Highland way

Jacobites saw the clans – an army of well-armed and trained men that could be raised in a matter of days – as their ace in the hole. However, even though the clan contingents were formed into regiments and the clan leaders given professional military titles, they were not soldiers. Their training was in how to 'lift' cattle and how to fight in clan struggles against enemies just like themselves. Raiding, an integral part of the upbringing and training of every fit Highland male, was, to the Lowland Scots and English alike, nothing more than theft. The perception was that the clansmen came down from the hills in search of cattle but lifted anything that took their fancy on the way. The fact that raiding was central to the function of the clan system was lost on those outside the Highlands. The complicated rules of raiding and pursuit, the necessity of the son of a chief proving himself by leading a raid, the concept of Highland honour, all of these meant nothing outside their own society. And little wonder, for by the eighteenth century most of Britain was becoming what we would nowadays recognise as modern, yet in the Highlands, though the bonds of its society were weakening, in some ways Highlanders still behaved little differently to their Iron Age ancestors.

Thus, while the Highlanders might be magnificent in battle, they were not like modern disciplined soldiers. Once a battle was won, or even once they were outside their own clan lands, their intention was always the same: to get their just reward for their endeavours! They were as unaware of the mores of modern society as modern society was of theirs. Amongst the Jacobites outside of the Highlands there were those who agreed with the Duke of Cumberland, that they were all savages, though to the Jacobite cause extremely useful savages. Highland ideas about how a man should behave were as impenetrable to Lowlanders and the English as the Gaelic language itself. Mutual incomprehensibility was guaranteed.

By the beginning of October 1715 the Earl of Mar had amassed about five thousand troops at Perth, preparatory to marching south. One of his commanders was John Sinclair, who held the rather grandiose title of the Master of Sinclair. Early on in the morning of Sunday 2 October, Sinclair was visited in Perth by an old friend, a merchant from Fife. The merchant had ridden through the night to bring news of a Government ship loaded with arms and ammunition at Burntisland. The cargo was intended for the Earl of Sutherland up in the north of the country, but the captain of the ship had made a brief stop in his home port to visit his family. The ship was scheduled to sail again on the tide that evening. Sinclair at once realised that this was a great opportunity to not only gather more arms and ammunition but to put one over on the enemy. So he went to see the Earl of Mar, with whom he did not always see eye to eye. The dithering Bobbing John refused to sanction a patrol being sent out. An hour later, at about eleven o'clock, Mar sent for Sinclair and further discussion took place. However, as usual, Bobbing John was having trouble making up his mind and it took a third meeting at noon before permission was given to go after the ship.

Mar, although by now convinced of the need for the raid, could not let pass the opportunity for a bit of petty spite. He sanctioned the raid but told Sinclair that he was to be in joint command with another officer, Harry Balfour. Sinclair, well aware of Mar's character, made no objection. After all, Balfour was a friend of his, and he knew they would get on fine. The pair of them organised eighty horsemen, leading fifty baggage horses, from Sinclair's own command, the Fife Squadron of Horse, but asked Mar to send out troops to cover their retreat. They would be going by Kinross, which was about twenty miles east of Stirling, and if the Duke of Argyll got word of the raid heading for the coast he would have time to organise a force from Stirling Castle to intercept the raiders. Yet again, Mar hummed and hawed, but, at last, he agreed to send a force of a hundred Highlanders to Kinross to guard the return journey. This force, under the command of Farquharson of Inverey, proved to be a bit of a handful.

At five o'clock in the evening, the patrol set off for Burntisland and managed to arrive there with no trouble. Once there, though, the news was not so good. The ship was not actually in the harbour but lay a little distance off shore. Sending a small group ahead to take control of the harbour mouth and to capture the ship's captain, Sinclair followed on a little later with the rest of his force. Everything went according to plan. They soon had control of the town and had captured the captain and commandeered enough small boats to row out and capture the ship.

Then things began to go wrong. A good breeze had blown up, an offshore breeze, and they had a great deal of trouble bringing the ship back into harbour. Tiring of waiting, the men posted around the town as sentries began to leave their posts. They were looking for drink and soon some of them began looting. The men supposedly looking after the baggage horses and even the party at the harbour, who were supposedly waiting to unload the ship's cargo, soon joined them.

Sinclair kept running around from position to position yelling at his men to attend to their duties. And this they did – until he was out of sight again – then off they would go for another drink. This was but a taste of things to come! The longer the ship took to come into the harbour the worse it got, and many of them were extremely drunk by the time they left Burntisland! At last, however, the ship was pulled into the dock and the unloading began. The haul was not as great as had been expected. There were only three hundred guns and a few barrels of gunpowder. Unloading them and getting them on the pack-horses was a slow job, and Sinclair and Balfour both had to help, so many of their men having disappeared into the town. Carousing could be heard from several directions as they roistered the night away!

While the raiders were still loading the horses, a messenger arrived from Auchtertoole, five miles back along the road to Kinross, where Farquharson and his men had arrived, their numbers now swollen to about five hundred. This was far more than Sinclair had asked for, and he thought he knew what had happened. Mar's Jacobite force had been sitting around at Perth effectively doing nothing for a month and so an extra four hundred Highlanders had come along with Farquharson, both out of boredom and in hopes of being able to do some personal looting!

Sinclair, having secured the weapons from the ship, had taken more from another vessel in the harbour. He had also taken the guns of the Burntisland Town Guard, who had not put up a fight. He then sent word to Farquharson to stay where he was. He was not needed in Burntisland. Once the weapons were all put on the horses, Sinclair headed back dragging many of his men from taverns and houses around the town. Some of them had disappeared off to have some drunken fun harassing a Presbyterian minister who had had the temerity to criticise them!

Coming to Auchtertoole Sinclair found only forty or so Highlanders. It was clear the rest had spread out over the surrounding countryside to see what they could gather in.

'Right men,' said Sinclair to the small band, 'some of you go out and bring in the rest of the men. We have work to do.'

This command was met with muttering and a lot of grim looks. These Highlanders wanted to join their fellows in looting, not stop them. A couple of them took such exception to Sinclair's orders that they levelled their cocked muskets at him, with muttered threats to shoot him.

Sinclair, though, was no fool or coward. He simply smiled broadly at them and said, 'Well, it's entirely up to yourselves lads, but I have had intelligence that there is a strong force of dragoons heading this way, so it might be better if we gather all our men in.'

Although he smiled as he said this, inside he was seething. He was a professional soldier and found the attitude of the Highlanders appalling, especially after what he had been through with his own men in Burntisland. Was there nobody who could be trusted to obey orders? he thought.

Hearing that there were dragoons about changed the Highlanders' attitudes instantly. The thought of a bit of drinking and looting was all very well, but if there was fighting to be done, they would be better off with as many of their friends as they could gather in. So, at Sinclair's words they immediately ran off in all directions, and it wasn't long at all before the whole force had rallied and were marching towards Kinross, with outlying scout patrols ahead and on either side of the main body. At the front of the force was Sinclair and his band of slightly less than eighty men with their baggage horses, and behind them, the raggle-taggle Farquharson's Highland contingent. Many of them, like some of Sinclair's horsemen, were carrying stolen bottles of drink, food and clothing, and, every so often, small groups would split off from the main force to ransack houses along the way. A great many of them by this time were at least half drunk. 'Thank God there aren't any dragoons coming,' thought Sinclair, or at least he hoped that was the case.

Bringing up their rear was a truly pathetic sight. It was a growing group of local people who had been subjected to the looting and were calling for the return of their belongings. Near Kinross Sinclair saw another force approaching. This was another group of Highlanders, under the command of Stewart of Invernytie, who had come from Perth with the same idea as the others. Sinclair rode slightly ahead when he saw them approaching and went straight up to Invernytie.

'We have been successful in our endeavours, Invernytie, but I have had word that there is a regiment of dragoons heading this way so I suggest we head back to Perth with all speed,' he said. Inverneytie agreed though he realised how disappointed his kinsmen would be to miss the chance for plunder, and the combined force headed back towards Perth. However, some of Farquharson's men and some of the Stewarts were dropping off in groups from the main column and continuing to loot any houses they saw. They had had little chance to make any gain from their endeavours in their time with the Jacobites and were making up for what they saw as lost time.

As for Sinclair, he was getting angrier by the minute, and as they got near to Perth he could control himself no longer. He turned to Invernytie, who was riding alongside him at the head of the column.

'You know, Invernytie, this simply will not do. Those poor people bringing up our rear have done us no harm. My God, Sir, they are our own people. We must halt this rabble and order them to hand back the goods they have stolen.'

Invernytie looked at Sinclair quizzically. 'Well, if you think you could do that you do not know our men, Sinclair. If you try to take what they have got for themselves they will turn on you, and I would not give a fig for you or your men's chances of survival,' he replied calmly.

Poor Sinclair was shocked. He could not see why Stewart's men would not do as they were ordered. Were they not soldiers in the army now? Calmly, Stewart tried to explain the Highlanders' concept of battle and raiding, but it was to little avail and by the time they got to Perth, Sinclair was even more furious. It was early evening when the raggle-taggle force arrived back in Perth. Sinclair at once went to Mar to give his report. He stated that the raid had been a success on one level but went on to complain bitterly about the behaviour of the men under the command of both Inverey and Invernytie. Sinclair saw the behaviour of the Highlanders as nothing but indiscipline. However, it seems that the events at Burntisland itself were glossed over. This caused even more friction with Bobbing John as Inverey was, of course, the lieutenant-colonel of Mar's own regiment. What was worse, word came to Balfour that some of the Highlanders were so incensed at the complaint laid against them that his life was in danger! From then on both he and Sinclair were always on their guard around the Highlanders. However, Sinclair was a fine soldier, and he realised that if he intended to fight on alongside the Highlanders in the Jacobite cause he could do little to control what he saw as savagery. He did, however, persuade Bobbing John that Highlanders should only ever be used under the control of their own officers, who were, in fact, their kin.

All in all, the Burntisland raid was one of the few high spots for the Jacobites in the '15; they had carried out a successful raid at no cost to themselves. Sinclair, however, never did adjust to the Highland concept of warfare.

Glengarry and the cuckoo

Not long after the Battle of Killiecrankie in 1715, a detachment of Government troops was sent south from Inverness to capture Invergarry Castle, the MacDonald stronghold on the western shore of Loch Oich. They were led by Captain Ramsay, who had a reputation as a brave man and a competent soldier. In the castle, the chief, MacDonald of Glengarry, had plenty advance warning that they were coming and was therefore on the lookout. He was keeping watch with the clan armourer Alistair MacDonald in a room at the top of the castle tower when he saw the troops come over the brow of a hill. Hanging on the walls of the room were several guns. Now, Glengarry was a man of considerable years and, like many of his peers, had a tendency to be a bit old fashioned. Where battle was concerned, and he was a famous warrior, he preferred to rely on cold steel, though he did carry pistols, which he had found useful. Their accuracy wasn't that great in the first place, and in the course of trying to use them during the Highlanders' preferred mode of attack, the downhill charge, they had often been shown to be ineffective.

In fact, Glengarry had often decried the guns as little more than 'sound and fury, signifying nothing'. Added to the muskets' questionable accuracy, they also had a tendency to blow up. Alistair, on the other hand, a man well versed in the use of such weapons, had often praised the efficiency of the long-barrelled guns, both in hunting and in battle. At the time one of the familiar terms used of these guns was *cuthag* or cuckoo.

Looking at the approaching troops, the chief turned to his companion and said, 'Well then, Alistair, now is your chance to show me if these pop-guns of yours are worth anything at all. See if you can bring down that officer at the head of those damned Redcoats.'

'Right, Glengarry, I will show you just what work this cuckoo can do, even at this distance.' And he took one of the pieces from its place on the wall. Just at that point Captain Ramsay moved from his position at the front of his men, back along the column of troops.

'Och, never mind him,' cried Glengarry, growing impatient, 'just see if you can shoot any of these damned Government men.'

By now Alistair had loaded and primed the gun in double quick time due to his years of practice, and he grunted as he leaned the barrel of the gun across the windowsill and took aim. A loud bang rang out, and almost immediately a red-coated soldier fell. Confusion broke out at the head of the column of troops showing that the musket ball had certainly found a mark.

'Ach, well done,' said Glengarry, patting Alistair on the back. 'The cuthag has certainly spat upon them.'

Alistair said nothing. He had a point to make. He simply took another gun from the wall, loaded and primed it and laid it across the windowsill. Again, he took aim, just as Captain Ramsay came down to the head of the column to see what was happening and to restore some semblance of order. Once more a loud bang rang out and the distant figure of the red-coated Captain threw up his hands and fell in the heather. The troops gathered round their fallen leader. He was dead. The musket ball had torn straight through his heart. They were being picked off one by one! It was still nearly a mile to Glengarry Castle. Who knew how many more would fall before they were close enough to mount a proper attack. And who could tell just how many wild Highlanders would come running, fully armed, to see what had caused the firing from the castle. The junior officer who was now in charge of the Government men, decided that, given the circumstances, discretion was very much the better part of valour. So, to Glengarry's great amusement the Redcoats picked up the body of their captain and headed back the way they had come. They didn't stop till they had gone all the way back to Inverness, many of them looking back over their shoulders just in case whoever had fired from the castle had decided to follow them.

From then on Glengarry had a great deal more respect for the 'cuckoos' that he had originally scorned as little more than fancy southern toys.

ESCAPES

A great escape

⟫⟩◆⟨⟪

In July 1718 James Stewart, the Old Pretender, as he was known to the Hanoverians, asked for the hand of Princess Clementina Sobieska in marriage. She was the granddaughter of the Polish king, John III Sobieski, a man renowned for having seen off the Turks at the siege of Vienna in 1683 and, in the eyes of many, saving Christian Europe from the infidels. The Polish royal family were, of course, Catholic, and Sobieski himself must have been perfectly well aware of what he was doing when he gave his consent to the marriage. Now, James had never seen Clementina at this stage, a not unusual circumstance amongst royalty at the time. She had been recommended to him by Charles Wogan, a trusted adviser who had been touring Europe on his behalf looking for a suitable bride. Wogan was a prominent Jacobite. Having been taken prisoner at Preston in 1715, he made a daring escape from Newgate prison the following year. Still only in his twenties, he had served for two years in Dillon's Regiment in the French Army and was a man of considerable talent and courage.

Now, when George I heard of the planned marriage he was furious. The last thing he wanted was the exiled Stewart claimant to the throne producing an heir! And the fact that by the standards of the time Clementina was a good catch only made things worse. Along with her royal pedigree, she would take a considerable amount of money, as well as the famous Sobieski jewels, with her when she went to Rome to marry James. James was in a winning situation and George was determined to stop the marriage happening any way he could. His first step was to try to get the Austro-Hungarian emperor, Charles VI, to put a stop to the marriage. Charles was not particularly keen to interfere in such matters, but, as he wanted to keep up good relations with the British crown, he rather reluctantly gave orders for the princess to be detained at Innsbruck. She was on her way to Rome when she was arrested and detained.

Both her father and her prospective husband immediately complained to Charles VI, but he appeared to be adamant that the marriage should not happen. He had made up his mind and would not be swayed from it. At this point the courage and commitment of the Stewarts and their followers came into play. James had no intention of being deprived of his bride, realising as he did that George was behind this. It was bad enough that the man was sitting on his throne, but for him to try and stop his marriage was just too much. Wogan, having already shown his abilities, was just the man to be sent to rescue the princess. So it was that in November 1718 Wogan turned up in Innsbruck posing as a French merchant. Like many Irish and Scots Jacobites of the time, he was fluent in several European languages and knew his way abut the Continent.

When he got there he found that Clementina, and her mother, were being kept in some comfort in the great medieval castle known as the Schloss Ambras. This great fortress was to test Wogan's abilities to the full. Back in Rome, as the months passed and no word came back, James began to despair of ever seeing his bride, but progress in Innsbruck was at least steady, if slow, and the redoubtable Wogan was getting on with things. Once he had laid his plans, he contacted the princess and her party and informed them of what he intended to do. The plan involved using several people so he left Innsbruck to collect together a group of trusted and capable Jacobite friends.

In April of the following year he returned to Innsbruck with his small but select party. There was his uncle, Major Gaydon, captains John Misset and Luke O'Toole from Dillon's Regiment and with them were Mrs Misset and her maid Janetta. The major and Mrs Misset were passed off as the Comte and Comtesse de Cernes. Janetta posed as their daughter; Wogan, as the Comte's brother; and Misset and O'Toole, as their servants. They took up residence in a high-class inn not far from the castle itself. The maid, Janetta, had been told that the group were hoping to rescue a young heiress whose father was attempting to stop her marrying Captain O'Toole, with whom she was deeply in love. Once everything had been arranged, Janetta was taken to the Schloss Ambras by Wogan. Here, they were met by Kotski, one of Clementina's pages, who brought Janetta into the castle in the evening with the explanation that she was the mistress of the steward of the schloss, Chateaudoux, a Frenchman, who was himself in on the plot. Wogan left the castle gate and took up a place in hiding nearby.

Clementina had been well briefed in advance by Kotski and earlier that evening she had complained of feeling unwell and retired to her bedroom saying that if the cold misty weather did not improve she was going to stay in her bed the following day as well. Her guards accepted this at face value and she went to her private room: after all, she was a princess, and they were used to obeying orders. Once there, she sat and wrote a letter to Charles VI. This was to explain that what she was doing was her own idea and that her mother had had no part in the proceedings. Once she had written and sealed the letter, she wasted no time in packing up her famous jewels and putting on a heavy fur-lined cloak. She then sat waiting. She did not have long to wait. Chateaudoux and

Janetta were shown into her room by Kotski. Janetta immediately got into the princess's bed – the emperor's men had instructions to check on her at least twice a day – and Clementina went into the room where her mother was.

'Mother, I am going now to meet my intended husband. The maid who will take my place has arrived, and before I go I want you to give me your blessing,' she said.

At this, both of them became rather emotional and there were hugs and kisses before the princess went on her way. Outside, Wogans' plans were unfolding nicely. Kotski went down to the front gate of the schloss with the princess, who wore Janetta's cloak over her own. Janetta was a bit bigger and taller than Clementina, but before arriving she had put on low-heeled shoes, and with Clementina wearing stylish high-heeled shoes the two appeared about the same height. With the princess also wearing two cloaks the deception passed off without a problem. Once they were through the gates of the schloss, Wogan came forward from where he had been hiding and the three of them scurried off to the nearby inn where the others were waiting. Kotski carried the parcelled up Sobieski jewels. Once they were at the inn, Clementina thanked Kotski profusely and he headed back to the schloss to make all seem as normal as possible. Then, Mrs Missett helped Clementina change into travelling clothes and the group headed off towards the border with the northern Italian republic of St Mark.

They were congratulating themselves that everything had gone like clockwork when Clementina realised something was missing. She had left the case of jewels back at the inn! Somebody would have to go back for them. Captain O'Toole volunteered, and, while the others waited freezing in the cold Alpine night, the Irishman rode back at breakneck speed to Innsbruck. It was still dark when he got there and O'Toole was reluctant to knock up the staff at the inn and alert them to the fact that his party had gone off in the night. He was a man of some considerable strength so he simply lifted the front door of the inn off its hinges and made his way silently into the building. He had no intention of striking a light and, in darkness, he gently felt his way to the room where the jewels has been left. Once he was in he groped about in the dark till he found the valuable parcel. At once he ran out of the door, leapt on his horse and took off southwards.

His companions were growing increasingly restive, beginning to imagine that the escape had been discovered and that O'Toole and the jewels had been captured. They heard the sound of hoofbeats. They all looked at each other, their hearts in their mouths. Had the alarm been raised and a company of guards sent to capture them?

'Och no, it's only the one horse,' said Wogan. With relief, 'it'll be O'Toole himself.'

Within seconds the truth of the statement was obvious and, once they had congratulated O'Toole, the small group of Jacobites headed off on their way. However, they were not yet home and dry for they still had many miles of the Austrian Tyrol to cross before they were safe beyond the border.

Back at Schloss Ambras the deception went well enough the following day, but by the next day the emperor's guards were becoming a little suspicious. At this, Kotski got Janetta out of the bed and showed her a tiny, damp and miserable little hole in the wall just outside the princess's apartments. She squeezed herself into this. The game was then up, for the next time the guards arrived it was clear to them that the princess had escaped. The castle was searched but Janetta wasn't found. Poor Kotski, however, fell under suspicion and ran off through the streets of Innsbruck. He was captured and dragged back to the castle.

Here, Clementina's mother produced her daughter's letter, and the upshot of it was that she was absolved of any blame. On hearing of the dramatic escape, Charles VI seems to have decided to hedge his bets. After all, the Jacobite cause might yet prove successful, and it certainly appears that he didn't pursue the fugitives with as much rigour as he might have.

However, one agent, who it seems was in the pay of the British Government, did head off after the fleeing group and arrived at the inn they were staying at the night before they intended crossing the border from Austria. O'Toole again stepped into the breach! He recognised the man from Innsbruck and struck up a conversation with him in the inn. He ordered up a bottle of wine and then another. Unknown to his companion, however, the wine, arriving in jugs, had been spiked with brandy by Mrs Missett, and by the end of the second bottle the man was so hopelessly drunk he was legless. Wogan was able to lead the party off to the border and safety with no further problems.

After all this adventure it would be fitting to say that the intended couple soon met and fell in love at first sight. In fact, James was in Spain by the time Clementina arrived in Rome. As ever, he was attempting to drum up support for his claim to the British thrones. This meant that the much longed for marriage was eventually carried out by proxy in Bologna, with Murray of Broughton standing in for James, and had to wait four months before being consummated. Clementina spent the time living with the Ursuline Nuns as the guest of the pope. Eventually, James returned. He landed on the Italian coast at Livorno on 27 August and met his bride a few days later on 1 September at Montefiascone. Here, the real wedding took place, blessed by the local bishop on direct orders from the pope. As for George I, he made his feelings clear in a letter to the emperor in which he expressed his displeasure and demanded that the emperor punish the

Sobieskis. Much good it did him! Charles VI thought it better to let things lie, and the Jacobite cause had a romantic and dramatic story to tell around the courts of Europe, which did their cause no harm at all.

A devoted wife

⇒◆⇐

In 1715 the Jacobites who rose in the north of England, under the inept and pathetic command of the Northumbrian aristocrat Thomas Forster, were joined by a force of Highlanders under the command of Mackintosh of Borlum and a group of Lowland noblemen. Amongst the latter group was William Maxwell, Fifth Earl of Nithsdale, a devout Catholic and a staunch Jacobite. After the farce of the siege of Preston and Forster's cowardly surrender, Nithsdale was taken, along with some of the other prisoners, to London to be tried for treason. He and his fellow peers were locked up in the relative comfort of the Tower of London to await trial.

On hearing of her husband's capture, Lady Nithsdale, who had been born Lady Winifred Herbert, daughter of the Marquis of Powys, headed south to London. By now it was December and her coach was stopped at Grantham by a heavy snowstorm. Now, Lady Nithsdale was generally considered by her friends to be rather frail, even if she had given birth to five children since marrying her husband in 1699. Whatever she lacked in bodily strength she more than made up for in steely determination. Pausing just long enough to have a couple of horses saddled, she set off in the snow for London on horseback along with her maid Cecilia Evans, another woman of strong character. Once in the English capital, Lady Nithsdale was allowed to freely visit her husband in the Tower, where he not only had his own room but was attended by his manservant, a far cry indeed from the conditions so many of the other prisoners suffered.

The trial started in January. The Government went through the motions of a fair trial, but there was never any doubt as to the verdict. All the defendants were found guilty. George I had only been on the throne for a year when the uprising took place and he was understandably paranoid about the strength of Jacobite feeling throughout Britain. As the events of the next half-century would make clear, there was a great deal of support for the Stewarts and he wanted to make an example of these particular rebels. The sentences handed down, however, were execution in a particularly sadistic manner. The specific sentence was delivered by Lord Cowper and it is worth including the full version.

The trial of Nithsdale and his companions took place in January. After the inevitable verdict of guilty was given, the judge declaimed, 'And now, my lords, nothing remains, but that I pronounce upon you (and sorry I am that it falls to my lot to do it) that terrible sentence of the law, which must be the same that is usually given against the meanest offender of the like kind. The most ignominious and painful parts of it are usually remitted by the grace of the crown to persons of your quality; but the law in this case being deaf to all distinctions of persons, requires that I should pronounce, and accordingly it is judged by this Court, that you, James, Earl of Derwentwater, William, Lord Widdrington, William, Earl of Nithsdale, Robert, Earl of Carnwath, William, Viscount Kenmure and William, Lord Nairn, and every of you, return to the prison of the Tower from whence you came; from thence you must be drawn to the place of execution and when you come there, you must be hanged by the neck, but not till you be dead; for you must be cut down alive, then your bowels must be taken out, and burnt before your face; then your heads must be severed from your bodies, and your bodies divided into four quarters; and these must be at the king's disposal. And God Almighty be merciful on your souls.'

Now, as soon as the horrific sentence was passed all sorts of influence-peddling took place to try and get the sentences reduced. Many people at the court who were staunch supporters of the House of Hanover thought that the execution of these men would strengthen the Jacobite cause. There were others who thought that, no matter how the rank and file were treated, it was too much to execute members of the nobility. After all, the crown might change hands again and the boot could well end up on the other foot!

Lady Nithsdale herself directly approached the king, literally throwing herself at his feet and clutching at the tail of his coat as she pleaded for her husband's life. George I, just a year into his reign, said nothing but kept walking and ended up dragging the unfortunate woman the length of one of the main rooms of the King's Apartments. She was eventually hauled away by two of the king's servants, the petition she had tried to stuff in his pocket falling to the floor. Many thought it a disgraceful scene and that the king had behaved badly, but then again the Hanoverian monarchs were never known for their good manners. As for Lady Nithsdale, she may have been greatly disappointed in the king's reaction but she was not a woman to accept defeat easily. Over the next few days many peers of the realm suggested clemency but the king was adamant: the rebels must feel the full force of the law.

The night before her husband's execution Lady Nithsdale turned up in a coach at the Tower of London with two companions. These were Mrs Morgan and Mrs Betty Mills, a tall, well-built lady, who appeared to be in the last months of pregnancy. Mrs Morgan was almost as tall but much slimmer, which just happened to allow her to be wearing two riding-cloaks without being noticed. By this time Lady Nithsdale was well known to the guards for she had been visiting her husband regularly and had been generous to the soldiers and jailers given the task of guarding the rebels. Prison warders expected to receive gratuities, and the soldiers on prison duty were also pleased to accept any gifts of money, particularly because of the sporadic nature of army pay. The three ladies were admitted to see Nithsdale for what was, to all intents and purposes, the second last chance that man and wife would have to see each other. But Lady Nithsdale had something else in mind.

The three ladies took turns to go into the small cell where Nithsdale was being kept. Being an aristocrat, it was not felt necessary that he should be kept in irons like a common criminal. As they took their turns, all of them chattering away nervously to the prisoner and among themselves, various articles of clothing were undone and handed over to the condemned man, who had had no advance warning of what was about to happen. Lady Nithsdale was in complete charge of the situation. While talking incessantly she used make-up she had brought with her to make her husband look as much like Mrs Mills as possible. As she herself later wrote, 'I had prepared some paint of the colour of hers, to disguise his hair as hers; and I painted his face with white and his cheeks with rouge, to hide his beard which he had not had time to shave.'

The guards, ill at ease listening to what they understood was the women taking their last farewells of Nithsdale, stood back from the room. The generosity of Lady Nithsdale on her previous visits had been appreciated, and they were truly embarrassed and a bit sympathetic towards the ladies. Once Nithsdale had been fully dressed and made up the next part of the plan came into effect. Mrs Morgan left first, soon followed by Mrs Mills. The guards had turned away from the harrowing scene of these ladies of quality sniffling and dabbing at their eyes with handkerchiefs. A short time later Lady Nithsdale came out, ushering her dressed up husband to the head of the stairs saying, 'Never mind my dear Betty, never mind. Just you get back to the house as quick as you can and get to your bed. We will just have to put our trust in the Lord. Now be off with you.' The embarrassed soldiers did not notice that there had now been three ladies leaving.

The rebel Lord scurried down the stairs while his wife went back to the door of the cell he had been occupying and went in. For several minutes she talked as if he was in the room, slowly becoming more emotional till at last she cried, 'I shall return later this evening my love, if they will let me through, and if they don't I will see you in the morning. Farewell,' and came out of the cell, clutching a handkerchief to her face and pulling the door closed behind her. She flitted past the guards and headed down the stairs. All this time Lord Nithsdale's manservant had been standing near the head of the stairs.

She went up to him and said, 'My Lord is at his prayers, do not disturb him,' and, calmly, she made her way downstairs and out of the Tower, finding a coach to take her back to her lodgings as the one in which she had come had already gone with its new occupant. It took several hours for the daring escape to be noticed, but once the word was out there was absolute uproar and many more soldiers were sent to the Tower to guard the other prisoners. A general warning went out to be on the look out for the escapee. There was, of course, no sign of him at his wife's lodgings, or at the homes of any of his friends. He was staying close to his wife in the home of a secret Jacobite sympathiser, who was not known as a friend of his. There was no way Nithsdale could try to return to Scotland: all the roads were being watched. Even if he could have gone home he would have been a fugitive with a price on his head for the rest of his days. There was no choice. He would have to leave the country.

Within a few days he was smuggled into the house of the Venetian ambassador by one of the ambassador's servants, a man called Michel, who was in the employ of the Jacobite court in Rome. A few days later, dressed in the livery of the ambassador's servants, Nithsdale rode down to Dover on the back of the official Venetian embassy coach, which contained the ambassador, who was going to meet his visiting brother. Here, it was a simple matter for Nithsdale to slip away and board a small boat that had been hired in advance by Michel to take him to Calais. The captain of the vessel had no idea who his passengers were, and, once out of the harbour, a good off-shore breeze sprung up. In fact, they made such good progress that the captain said to his passengers, 'Aye, this is a fair wind indeed, it could have done you no better if you had been fleeing for your lives.' The two gentlemen merely smiled and nodded politely!

As for Lady Nithsdale, after being closely questioned by Government agents, she was allowed to go free and returned to Scotland. Here, she stayed just long enough to gather up a substantial amount of money and important legal documents before returning south and crossing the Channel to join her husband at Lille. They carried on together to the Jacobite Court in Rome. Here, Nithsdale was made a Knight of the Thistle by the man he considered James III of England and VIII of Scotland, although if there was hero in this affair it would appear to have been his wife! In fact, as public sympathy towards the Jacobites grew, women's cloaked hoods became known as Nithsdales in honour of the lady's brave and gallant actions.

Seton's escape

⇒◆⇐

George Seton, Fifth Earl of Wintoun, was an unusual man. In his youth he tired of the aristocratic life, and his activities led to a falling out with his family. He decided to travel and set out for the Continent without informing his family where he was going. He was well educated, could live on his wits and he was not afraid of hard work. George spent several years in France, where he worked for a considerable time as a sort of apprentice to a blacksmith and bellows-maker. Despite his aristocratic upbringing, he had never been afraid to get his hands dirty. This period in his life gave him a fund of stories with which he would later entertain his fellow Jacobites on campaign and, later, in prison. All the while he was in France he neglected to keep in touch with his direct family. So, when his father, Viscount Kingston, passed away, the family decided to let the next heir to the titles and estates take his place. Now George might have been eccentric, but he was no fool, and he had been kept up to date with what was happening back home by a servant who knew how to keep a confidence. So, just when the new earl was about to take up his position, who should turn up but George, back from his travels and ready to take over as the fifth Earl of Wintoun. His family were upset by this, but, as there was no doubt he was the legitimate heir, they could do nothing to stop him taking up the title and setting up home at the family estate in East Lothian. The Setons were traditionally Jacobites so when the 1715 Rising happened he was already inclined to take up arms on behalf of the Stewart cause.

However, his involvement with the cause was hastened and assured when the local Lothian militia stepped in. One day in 1715, they arrived at his home in Seton overlooking the Firth of Forth while he was out. Having heard that the Jacobites had raised their standard in support of the Old Pretender, they arrived with their minds made up that Seton was one of the rebels and that he would have to pay the price. They stormed through his ancestral home and then proceeded to desecrate the chapel where his ancestors were buried. He later said that the militia went as far as opening up the sepulchres in the chapel and desecrating the corpses in them, slashing at them with swords and scattering the bones of his forefathers around the chapel. There is little doubt that there was a great deal of personal resentment against Seton behind this barbarous behaviour. The effect was that George, whatever his earlier intentions, was now firmly on the side of the Jacobites, and he wasted no time.

He sent word round those he knew were loyal to the cause in Lothian and soon had a substantial body of armed horsemen with him at Seton. This troop then set off to join with the Northumbrian Jacobites under the pathetic leadership of Thomas Forster, MP for Northumberland and Earl of Derwentwater. Forster was given command of the combined force because he was the only Protestant noble amongst them. The alternative might have been to let Mackintosh take control but the Englishmen were most likely reluctant to do so. Centuries of stories about the wild and savage Highlanders made them wary. Forster and the other English insurgents were set on marching south into England, but Seton and Mackintosh of Borlum, who arrived at Kelso with more than a thousand armed Highlanders, wanted to secure the border towns and lay plans to attack the Duke of Argyll at Stirling.

The two parties disagreed so strongly that Seton and his men headed north. They were pursued by a messenger, who pleaded with the earl to return to Forster's command. He listened for a while then stood silent for longer. At last, he spoke, 'It shall never be said to future generations that the Earl of Wintoun deserted King James's interests or his country's good.' Then, taking a grip of his own ears, he said to the messenger, 'You, or any man, shall have liberty to cut these off my head if we do not all repent it.'

So, he went back to join Forster's command, but from this time on he was kept out of the loop when it came to making decisions. He was also treated badly by Forster, who seems to have taken a fit of pique towards him, even though he had returned to serve under his command. However, he had committed himself to the plan of action and he stuck with it. The Highlanders too went along with Forster's plan with a great deal of reluctance. At first things went well and the Jacobite force was welcomed in Lancaster. Forster insisted they press on as he was sure that many of the population of Lancashire would rise to join them as they continued south-wards. As in many other things, he was dead wrong. The fiasco ended with surrender after the Jacobites were briefly besieged in the town of Preston and it seems likely that Forster was lucky to escape a Highland dirk after his craven surrender of his command to the Government troops after the short-lived siege. While there is no doubt he was greatly disappointed that more English Catholics and Episcopalians did not rally to his support, and became convinced that victory was impossible, the Highlanders thought him no more than a coward, and effectively a traitor to the cause. Of course, when the troops were surrendered to General Wills at Preston, Seton was one of them, and he was soon transported to the Tower of London to await trial for treason.

He was brought to trial before the House of Lords on 15 March 1716, and there he defended himself, but he must have known that this was no more than a show trial. His arguments were dismissed out of hand by the chief judge, Lord Cooper.

'I hope,' the earl said at that point, 'you will do me justice, and not make use of Cowper-law, as we used to say in our country: hang a man first and then judge him after.'

This hardly enamoured him to the bench, but as the verdict was preordained it made no difference. He was found guilty of treason and, as a member of the peerage, he was sentenced to be beheaded on Tower Hill. Now, although he had had an interesting and complicated life thus far, George Seton was still only in his mid twenties and had no intention of meekly succumbing to his sentence. While to outward appearances he was resigned to his fate and kept his fellow peers amused during daylight hours with tales of his life as a humble blacksmith, once night fell George took on a different aspect. Somehow, probably by bribing one of the guards – as prisoners effectively had to provide their own food they were allowed their own money, and that was something George was not short of – he managed to get his hands on some basic tools, including a small hammer and chisel and a saw. In the nights leading up to his execution he made good use of the skills he had picked up while living in France. Very carefully and quietly he began to saw through the bars on the window of the cell. Once they were cut through he could work them loose with the hammer and chisel. One at a time he cut through the bars, replacing them at the end of each night, till enough were cut through to allow him room to crawl out of the window and on to the nearby walkway. From there, with all the aplomb of one born into the aristocracy, he simply walked down the stairs and out of the Tower of London, supposedly the most impregnable prison in England.

Once he was free of the Tower, he made his way into the City of London and presented himself to one of his friends whom he knew was sympathetic to the Jacobite cause and waiting for the chance to prove it. From there it was a relatively simple matter for him to disguise himself and make his way by ship to France. From France, George found no problem in moving on to the Jacobite court at Rome, where he was greeted as something of a hero for his daring escape. The title of the Earl of Wintoun was abolished after his escape. Seton spent the rest of his life in Rome, where he died in 1749 after witnessing yet another failed Jacobite attempt to regain the British thrones.

Breakout

⥤◆⥢

After the disaster at Preston all the leaders of the Jacobite force were transported to London for trial. Among them was Mackintosh of Borlum, who had shown his worth as a soldier by crossing the River Forth under the noses of English ships with a thousand troops to join the southern Jacobite force under Thomas Forster, Earl of Derwentwater. Mackintosh, like his men, many of whom were his own kin, had been outraged by Forster's surrender to the Government troops. They had wanted to fight on, and, at the very least, have the chance to fight their way clear of Preston and head back to Scotland. Instead, Forster's disgraceful cowardice had ensured that many of them were executed and large numbers of them were transported to the West Indies, never to see their beloved Highlands again.

At this time Borlum was in his early sixties, but he was still fit and strong. A tall, fair-haired man, he was intelligent and cultured, but, when it came to battle, he had a reputation for being as stubborn as a mule and as savage as a tiger. On being transported to Newgate prison in London he immediately began thinking about how to effect his escape. In fact, as early as 11 April, one of the Jacobite prisoners had managed to escape. This was Thomas Forster himself, who had made off using a duplicate key in the middle of a drinking session with the governor of Newgate prison, Mr Pitt. This escape was so slickly organised and carried out that there were those who said that the Government themselves were behind it. It seems the authorities might have been a little reluctant to publicly try a man who was both an MP and a Protestant for fear of the effect on public opinion. Borlum, a well-liked and respected soldier, often referred to as the 'Old Brigadier', didn't have to rely on secret Government connivance to get out of Newgate.

Now, during the day prisoners were generally free to wander round the courtyard that lay behind the great locked gates of the prison. One of the gates, however, had a door in it to allow people to get in and out without the huge gates having to be swung open, a manoeuvre that entailed clearing the courtyard of the prisoners. In the course of a normal day, turnkeys, soldiers, members of the families of the non-political prisoners, and a variety of tradesmen came and went through this door. It was always guarded, but sometimes by no more than a turnkey and a couple of soldiers. Beyond the gate lay the teeming streets of London, constantly thronged with people, carts and coaches.

On the evening of 4 May, a large group of the Jacobite prisoners, numbering nearly sixty, were dining together with a fair amount of wine and punch being consumed. They all seemed to be merry and remarkably happy considering their circumstances, and the guards thought little of it when they gathered in the press-yard, the area behind the gate, supposedly to get some fresh air. Borlum, however, had more than fresh air on his mind and had already discussed the possibilities with some of his compatriots, including his son and his brother, who had both been captured with him at Preston, and the redoubtable Charles Wogan, who had rescued Princess Clementina Sobieski. There were only a couple of turnkeys guarding the gate when Mackintosh shouted in Gaelic, 'Right lads, let's get at them!'

Before they could react the men at the gate were overpowered by Borlum and half a dozen others. The keys were stripped from their belts, the door in the gate flew open and the whole group of Jacobite prisoners steamed out into the street. Borlum and his helpers at the gate knew exactly where they were going. He had been in London on several occasions and knew his way around. Once they had reached the first corner they slowed down and walked calmly to a house just a few streets away that was owned by a Jacobite sympathiser. Within a couple of days Borlum and his son travelled to Ipsden Bassett in Oxfordshire, where his sister lived with her husband, Thomas Reade, the local squire. Here they stayed till arrangements could be made for a passage to France. Sadly, Borlum's brother was later recaptured at Rochester. Behind them, the others, some having had too much wine or punch, spread out through the streets around the prison. Many of them had no idea of where they were going and over the next couple of hours were rounded up by soldiers. Some of them were simply found after having asked directions, their Scottish accents giving them away, while others were seen running away from the jail, noticed by the crowds in the street, who informed the pursuing soldiers. A few others were simply too drunk to get far and missed their chance. In all, about a dozen of the prisoners managed to escape successfully alongside Old Borlum.

One of these was Robert Hepburn of Keith. Like many of his co-prisoners, he had had no idea that Borlum was going to try and break out – some said Borlum himself only decided at the last minute – but he was happy to seize the opportunity. By the time he was in the street outside the prison, Borlum and his party had already disappeared, so Hepburn just ran. A few minutes later he realised he was lost. He knew that his wife and family had come down to London and were living near the prison, but how could he find them in this warren of streets? If he asked any kind of directions he would show himself to be a Scot, and behind him he could already hear the soldiers searching through the streets. As he walked briskly along, his heart thumping and his mind racing, he looked up at a house he was passing. At first he could not believe his eyes. There in the window was a large and ancient pewter plate that he had seen many times before. It was the Keith Tankard and had been in his family for generations! At once he hammered on the door of the house, and it was opened by none other than his wife! It was an emotional and tearful reunion. Once they had calmed down they sat down together, and he learned that she had rented this house under a false name to be near to him. She had tried many times to get to see him but without success. Lying low for a couple of days, the Keith family then followed Borlum's example and found safety in France.

The escape from Newgate was not the end of the adventures of William Mackintosh of Borlum. While living in France he was active in Jacobite affairs, like many of his countrymen, longing for the chance to return to Scotland and try again. In 1719 the chance did come again, and Borlum landed at Stornoway in April with the regiment of Spanish soldiers who had come to support another rising. This attempt at Jacobite rebellion was notable for even worse planning and leadership than the '15. After utter ineptitude from the Jacobite command at the battle of Glenshiel, the Spanish soldiers surrendered, and when they were transported to Edinburgh Castle Borlum was with them. Why he had not simply faded away into the Highlands in the chaos at the end of the battle is a mystery. Perhaps his sense of honour prevented him from deserting the Spanish commander, Don Nicolas Bolano, in his hour of need.

Once they were in Edinburgh, having given their parole, a promise to fight no more, the Spanish officers were given the liberty of the town. There was a bit of scandal when it transpired that they were not even being fed and had to rely on local Jacobite sympathisers for food and other necessities, but they were returned to Spain in October. Parole, however, was not a privilege extended to Borlum. Having already escaped once and then having had the temerity to come out again in the Jacobite cause, he was tried, found guilty and sentenced to be imprisoned in Edinburgh Castle for life. In those times that meant life; he was to stay there till he died in 1743. However, although his body was imprisoned his mind was not, and during the long years of his imprisonment he wrote and had published several works on improvements in agriculture, a topic of consuming interest at the time. All who knew him spoke highly of William Mackintosh, and the fact he was never released, when so many others were pardoned, even now suggests little more than venomous pique on the part of the British Government.

Thriepland

⟫◆⟪

In 1715 Sir David Thriepland of Fingask, near Perth, and his son, also David, came out with Mar. Young David was sent with the troops led by Mackintosh of Borlum to help with the rebellion in the north of England. However, getting from the main Jacobite army at Perth to the north of England was not an easy task. The Duke of Argyll, leader of the Hanoverian cause in Scotland, had a considerable number of troops south of Stirling, and the preferred option of crossing the Firth of Forth by boat was complicated by the fact that there were three English men-o-war in the estuary. Mackintosh was a capable and intelligent leader and decided that he would divide his troops, two thousand five hundred of them, into two groups. The smaller group, some five hundred, were instructed to go to Burntisland and act as if they were going to embark on a crossing of the firth from there. The rest of the men, David Thriepland among them, headed off to the more eastern ports of the East Neuk – Crail, Elie and Pittenweem – where a fleet of small craft had been assembled in advance. The plan was for the men at Burntisland to draw the warships to them and, once the tide was running against them, the ships would have great difficulty in trying to intercept the main contingent rowing their way.

The Burntisland contingent launched a few boats while others built defensive banks for the cannon they had with them. The warships came in and attacked them, and soon there was a heavy firefight going on between the shore batteries and the ships. This went on through the night, and at dawn, once the tide had turned, Mackintosh set out with his flotilla of small boats. Most of the boats had made it more than halfway across when the English ships realised what was happening. Using all of their seamanship, the captains of two of the ships began to work their way against the tide towards the Jacobite fleet. The last eight boats, full of men from the Earl of Strathmore's regiment, realised that they were in danger of being caught and headed for the ancient, holy Isle of May. Here, they landed and built trenches, expecting the warships to come and attack them. Luckily this didn't happen, and the following day they simply rowed back to Fife unmolested. Meanwhile, most of the rest of the boats had made it to the Lothian shore at North Berwick, Aberlady and Gullane, with only a couple of stragglers still out in the firth. David Thriepland was in one of these and as the English ships grew ever closer it was obvious that he could not escape. There was no point in trying to either flee or to fight. The warships could simply blow their boats out of the water with their cannons. So, the last two boats, with about forty men, were taken by the naval ships and their crews disarmed and put below decks under armed guard.

The rest of the Jacobite forces mustered on the shore and set off eastwards towards Edinburgh. The English ships took their prisoners into the Port of Leith, still held by a small force of Redcoats, and they were locked up, under armed guard, in the tolbooth, or jail. This was not what Thriepland had planned for himself. However, he didn't have long to wait before Borlum's men marched in from the east and took Leith with little or no bother. The main body of Government troops was with Argyll, coming from Stirling towards the capital, which was now threatened by Borlum. It was with a great sense of relief that Thriepland and his companions found themselves being freed to rejoin their comrades. Having liberated the prisoners, Borlum's next step was to liberate the contents of the Customs House in Leith. This consisted of a large amount of provisions and, even more welcome, a liberal amount of brandy! Over the next few days Borlum and Argyll made feints and marches between Leith and Edinburgh, neither one feeling he had enough of an advantage to launch an all-out attack. It was during this period that David Thriepland, on a scouting patrol towards the capital, came across a much larger force of Redcoats and was once more taken prisoner. He certainly seemed to be having no luck in his military endeavours. He was taken back to Edinburgh and here he was locked up in the city tolbooth.

A few days later, he was taken from the tolbooth and transferred to the castle, and he heard on the way that Borlum and his force had marched off southward. There now seemed to be little hope of another rescue! In the castle he was put into a large room with half a dozen of his fellow Jacobites. The room had no bars on its window as it was set in a sheer wall about thirty feet above the narrow path running along the castle rock below. On the other side of the path was another sheer drop more than twice as high. Anyone trying to get out of the window would probably fall and be lucky to escape with his life, never mind injury. This path, though, was a place where the local citizenry were wont to take a stroll along Castle Hill, and one day, looking down, he saw a group of four young ladies whom he had met several times at social gatherings in the capital. Two of them, sisters, he was sure, were from a family who were staunch Jacobites. He ran to his cell door to check there were no guards in the immediate vicinity and whistled to the ladies. He then waved them over as close as they could come to his cell window. Their reactions were a trifle foolish. They whispered and giggled to one another before coming closer.

Holding a finger to his lips, in a stage whisper he said, 'Wheesht,' trying to control the lassies. They were both excited and intrigued by the situation. Here was young David Thriepland, a hero to those of the Jacobite persuasion in the city, and, as one of the more eligible young bachelors in their social circle, someone of more than passing interest to them. And he was apparently seeking their help.

This was high adventure and enough to get their hearts pounding. David was at a bit of a loss. The lassies were about twenty feet below him, and if he tried to speak to them there was a strong likelihood that he would be overheard. Frantically using hand signals, he tried to let them know what he wanted. This pantomime caused two of them to start giggling, but he could see that the older two girls were paying close attention. He repeated his actions then waited for the two older ones to nod, showing that they understood what he was trying to convey. All four then hurried away, the two younger ones still giggling and looking back over their shoulders as they disappeared out of his sight.

When they were gone he stood there his own heart racing. Did they understand? Would they do what he wanted? More importantly would any of them want to report him to the authorities? He was pretty sure that the two oldest girls could keep the others under control, and he had little doubt of their loyalties. Still, he was asking a lot of a group of young girls still in their mid to late teens. What ifs swirled round his head and his breathing got shorter. There were just too many imponderables. All he could do was to wait and see what happened. He tried to stop thinking about it all and calm down. Breathing deeply, he sat on his bed and told himself to relax. At last he calmed down.

Later that night he was standing by his window coiling and uncoiling the long, strong cord he had managed to pick up on one of the occasions he had been let out to stroll along the battlements.

His guards had been busy discussing some situation in a local tavern the night before and he had taken his chance to lift the cord. His heart was pounding as he looked out of the window at the path below. Then, suddenly, there was a shadow moving. And another. And another. Three of the lasses had returned. Silently, in the pale light of the stars they waved to him. 'Thank you, Lord,' he whispered under his breath. He threw the cord down. Thankfully it was long enough. He felt a tug as one of the girls took the end. Below him the indistinct figures bent over the cord. Then came another tug and he pulled up. Over the next ten minutes he pulled up a more than a dozen blankets and pulled them into the cell. By now his cell-mates had realised that something was happening and were standing round him as he pulled. They needed no bidding. As the blankets came in to the cell they were passed from eager hand to eager hand. After he pulled the last blanket through the window, David leaned out and waved his thanks to the vague figures below. They waved back and he thought, for a moment, that one of them had blown him a kiss. He smiled at the thought then turned to the matter in hand.

It was only a matter of half an hour or so before the pile of blankets was torn into strips then twisted and tied into a strong rope more than thirty feet long. Tying one end to a large wooden table, they threw the other end out of the window. In absolute silence, by the dim flickering light of the one oil lamp in the cell, one by one the young men climbed out of the window and down the rope to the path below. Once they were all on the path below, David led them round the side of Castle Hill and down into the city, every hair on his neck standing up as he expected at any moment to hear a shout from the castle. Keeping to the shadows, they made their way down to the Nor Loch, and then headed north away from the capital.

Travelling through the night, they headed towards Stirling. The following day, after a short rest, they carefully made their way west, keeping off the main road and using the cover of hedgerows and woods as much as possible. Luckily, David had friends near Falkirk who gave them food, and they carried on the following night and day, heading for the ancient passage across the Forth at the Fords of Frew. In the evening of the third day, they were hiding out in a lint mill on a farm near the Fords of Frew when their lookout called, 'Redcoats coming.'

They looked out of the windows to see a large group of Redcoats carrying muskets coming through the farmyard towards the mill. Someone had clearly informed the soldiers of their presence.

'Right lads,' said David quietly, 'get out through the windows at the back and I'll slow them up.'

As the others dropped out of the windows and ran to the west, David calmly took out his flint and steel and, piling a heap of lint on the floor of the mill, struck a spark. At once the lint roared into flame and he piled more and more lint on to the flames. Soon he had a blaze going and smoke began to drift out of the windows. He could still clearly see the Redcoats through the thickening smoke. They had stopped. They had no intention of entering a burning building! Waiting till the last possible moment, as the blaze began to take hold of the wooden structure, David ran to a window at the back and jumped out, rolling over as he landed. He picked himself up and ran across the fields to where he could just make out his friends behind a hedge. Behind him the lint-mill roared into flame, the smoke swirling thickly around the farmyard. The Redcoats on the far side retreated from the blaze, and David and his friends took their chance to put a good distance between them and the troops. Later that night they crossed the Forth and headed off towards Perth, where David and his companions rejoined the Jacobite army.

The Ogilvies

Many of the stories told of the Jacobites have attracted those of a romantic disposition. None are more remarkable than the tale of the Ogilvies, the earls of Airlie. James, Lord Ogilvy, the eldest son of the third earl, was out in the '15 and again thirty years later, by which time his younger brother John had taken over the earldom and his nephew David had become one of the foremost Jacobites of his day. David and his wife were notable not just for their loyalty to the Jacobite cause but for their courage and tenacity. When Prince Charlie raised his standard at Glenfinnan, David Ogilvy, eldest son of the current earl, gathered around eight hundred men from the Braes and Glens of Angus and marched with them from the head of Glen Clova over the mountain path known as the Capel Mounth to join the cause. Now, the family were playing a not uncommon but dangerous game. Ostensibly the earl himself, by not joining his son, could claim to be loyal to the House of Hanover. So, no matter the outcome they would have somebody in the winning side. The landed families of Scotland, like the clans so many of them derived from, always had a much stronger loyalty to their own kin than any king, whether in Edinburgh or London.

The Angus men were with Charlie through the march to Derby and the long retreat north, and they suffered heavy casualties at Culloden. After that crushing defeat, Ogilvy marched remnants of his regiment back to Milton of Glen Clova, where they disbanded, each to try and survive as he might. For many years after this there was a small garrison of Government troops at Clova, but the locals, despite their presence, still held their annual Highland games – the men in Highland dress and carrying arms – high up on the plateau above the glen at a place still known as the Bowling Green.

As for David Ogilvy, he knew better than to try and return to the family home of Cortachy near the foot of Glen Clova. It had been occupied by Hessian troops brought over from Hanover to bolster the British Army. He was well known, and his chances of avoiding capture in Scotland were remote. Cumberland's troops had stopped off at Glamis on their way north to Culloden and had had a taste of how the locals thought of them one night. A large company of dragoons, on overnight stand-by, found that each and every one of their saddle-girths had been cut. Angus was fervent Jacobite country!

Now, David realised his best hope was to fly to France, where he hoped he could be joined by his wife, the noted beauty Margaret Johnstone, who had accompanied him on the campaign. Though she, too, was in danger, he knew that if he was caught he would pay the ultimate price, his life. He therefore decided to head to Dundee, where he hoped he would find a sympathetic, or greedy, captain to sail him to France or, failing that, somewhere on the Continent.

He set out, after the regiment disbanded, with one companion, a servant called John Thompson, who was to prove a staunch and capable friend. It was thought best that David disguise himself in some way as there were certainly many Government spies about, and the two of them hit on the plan of exchanging roles, with Thomson acting as master and David as servant. This caused a bit of a problem for in those days it was the custom in Scottish inns to cook one's own food. In a tavern near Kirriemuir, Ogilvy tried to make porridge for the pair of them. He didn't have a clue how to do it, and he kept throwing more and more handfuls of oats in to the pot that was bubbling on the fire. Thompson was clearly exasperated by this and hissed at him, 'Twinkle your little finger my lord, twinkle your little finger,' trying to instruct him to stir the porridge with the wooden spirtle. He was overheard by two or three people sitting around the main room of the inn and a character who had been sitting at a nearby table at once got up and left. Thompson realised that the man was probably off to inform the nearest soldiers he could find, so the pair of them quickly ate the very lumpy porridge and headed off westwards to throw any possible pursuit off their intended trail. They headed to Lintrathen, where Ogilvy hid with a sympathetic farmer. Thompson then headed on his own to Dundee to try and arrange passage abroad. David spent an anxious week hiding out on the farm as Government troops searched the area for him, but at last Thompson came back to report that suitable arrangements had been made. The two of them, still in their adopted roles, went down through the villages of Airlie and Glamis and passed through the Sidlaw Hills at Lumley Den. They then walked on to Broughty Ferry, now part of Dundee, where a ship was soon to set sail for Bergen, in Norway. David would rather have gone straight to France but realised that he would be pushing his luck by waiting around for a suitable ship. They were only one step ahead of the pursuit, and no sooner had they set sail for Bergen than the authorities found out about it. Their ship stopped, first in Jutland and upon arrival in Bergen, and Ogilvy was arrested as soon as his feet touched the harbour dock. Word that a criminal sought by the British Government was landing at Bergen had been sent by fast ship to the relevant authorities. However, the faithful Thompson was not arrested, and, with the application of a little gold and the assistance of a couple of Jacobite sympathisers amongst the local

Scottish traders, it was a relatively simple matter for him to arrange Ogilvy's escape. In the dead of night, David slipped from the prison in Bergen, and there was Thompson with a pair of horses to whisk them off to Gothenburg, in Sweden, where they had no trouble in getting a passage to France. David went on to serve in the French Army with his own regiment, made up of exiled Scots and Irish.

David Ogilvy was seen as a real hero by the Jacobites and was a handsome man, a brave soldier and generally a pretty attractive character. His escapes from under the noses of the Government were a morale boost to the despondent Jacobites and a considerable blow to the Hanoverian Government. However, he wasn't the only notable Ogilvy in the '45.

His wife, Lady Ogilvy, born Margaret Johnstone of Auchterhouse, was not only an outstanding beauty but, as her actions showed, she was also a woman of remarkable strength of character. She was one of the belles of the ball at Prince Charles Edward Stewart's short-lived court in Edinburgh, and she accompanied the Jacobite army on its ill-fated foray into England. In fact, it is said she was such a brave woman that she thought little of standing on the battlefield holding the reins of a spare horse for her husband in case he needed it. During the retreat from Derby she was sent ahead of the main body of troops in a coach with a substantial mounted escort. Somehow a rumour started that the coach in fact contained the prince and a great deal of gold! This was probably the cause of the attack on the coach that took place at Lancaster, in which three people were killed. The assailants, not Government troops, were driven off, and Margaret was unharmed. Now, at this time both the Government and the Jacobites had extensive intelligence networks throughout England and Scotland, and on their way north Lady Ogilvy's party heard that there was another ambush planned near Perth. It seemed that someone with the party was sending information ahead of them so she returned to the main body of the army.

On their way north, in January 1746, the Jacobite army laid siege to Stirling Castle. An army led by General Henry Hawley was approaching from the south. Most of the Jacobite army set off to meet the approaching forces and had their last victory, such as it was, at the Battle of Falkirk on the 17th. After this, they headed north, picking up the troops besieging the castle as they went. Nobody, however, told Lady Ogilvy what was happening, and she woke up a couple of days later in the inn where she was staying to find the town of Stirling filling up with Hawley's troop, who had re-formed, and, having been reinforced with more troops, were following the Jacobite army. Her coach was outside the inn, and, still in bed, she could hear the sound of a troop of Government soldiers surrounding it. As quick thinking as she was brave, she moved quickly and headed out of the back of the inn and along the road out of town. She had dressed herself in the spare clothes of her maid, leaving her own rich dresses hidden under a bed. Luckily, she also had some money, and soon she and her maid had managed to get themselves horses and were riding off after the Jacobite army. We can imagine the words she had with her husband for abandoning her to the not so tender mercies of the Government troops.

On 16 April 1746 she was on Drumossie Moor, once more holding a spare horse for her husband, when the unfortunate tactics of the prince and his advisers led the Jacobites into the hellish slaughter of Culloden. Once the battle was lost she headed off to a friend's house not far away but was soon identified and captured. Probably because of her status, she was not subjected to the brutality that so many Scots women underwent at the hands of the Government forces and was sent to the prison in Inverness.

Prisons in those days, as now, were grim places. While there she heard the uplifting news that her husband had managed to escape to the Continent. After two months here she was escorted to Edinburgh, where at least she would be more comfortable in the castle than in Inverness prison. As a notable aristocrat, and one who had played such an important role at the prince's court, the Government intended making an example of her. They didn't, however, allow for her courage and intelligence.

While she was locked up in Edinburgh Castle Lady Ogilvy was visited regularly by her sister Barbara, who lived in Edinburgh. Barbara had arranged for a local woman to handle Lady Ogilvy's laundry, and she was soon a regular sight going back and forth from the castle. She had an assistant, a young lass who carried the laundry up to the castle gate for her, but was not allowed in. The laundress herself was an older woman who had been born with a twisted back and walked with a very pronounced limp. One time, after delivering the clean laundry, she was about to leave the cell when Lady Ogilvy spoke.

'You have a strange way of walking, would you mind if I tried to walk the same way?' she asked with a smile.

'Well, if it pleases your Ladyship, I can see no harm in it,' replied the bemused laundress, thinking to herself, 'It's right enough what they say about the nobility, they are gey queer.'

So, over the next few visits Lady Ogilvy was coached in how to limp like the laundress. She then broached her plan to the laundress and asked her to smuggle in a spare set of her own clothes amongst the laundry over the course of the next week.

A day or so later, in the evening, when the warden came to Lady Ogilvy's cell with a servant carrying her evening meal, he met Barbara at the door of her sister's quarters.

'I am sorry.' She said. 'My sister is unwell. She does not want any food. If you don't mind, I will stay here tonight and keep her company. She really isn't well at all.'

The warden agreed to let her stay. Barbara went back in the cell, and he heard her whispering to her sister. Barbara then came back to the cell door and quietly wished the warden a good night. In the morning, when her breakfast was brought, Barbara said she had had a bad night but had fallen asleep and seemed to be more peaceful now. It wasn't until the following day, a Monday, that the truth was discovered. The guards on the gate of the castle had not noticed that two limping maids had gone down the hill on the Saturday evening – and why should they? It had been carefully arranged that Lady Ogilvy, dressed in the laundress's clothes and feigning her limp and hunched way of walking, would go out of the castle first, and the old woman would follow after the guard on the gate was changed.

Lady Ogilvy had simply changed into the laundress's clothes, pulled the shawl over her head, lifted the laundry basket and hobbled her way down to the gate to join the young lass outside the castle. None of the guards paid any attention to the crippled figure passing by them, and, once the pair of them were clear of the castle, they turned into one of the many wynds leading off the High Street and disappeared from view. The young lass was a bit taken aback at her mistress's silence as she was normally keen to chat about her visits to Lady Ogilvy. You can imagine her surprise when, once they were a fair distance from the castle, the old crooked lady whipped off her shawl and stood up, revealing herself to be a graceful and beautiful young woman. She took the young lass's hand and pressed some silver coins into the astounded young girl's hand. Then she spoke.

'Now, you will not tell anyone of this, will you? Your mistress said you were a fine lass and that I can count on you.'

The lassie could only nod agreement, being totally lost for

words. Lady Ogilvy smiled at her companion, winked broadly, and ran off! She then made her way down the Royal Mile to a friend's house in Abbey Hill, where a set of men's clothing and a horse were waiting for her, as was her personal maid. Lingering only long enough to say farewell to Lady Ogilvy's faithful friends, the pair of them set off south. They did not take the road to London, where the chances of being recognised and arrested were considerable, as Lady Ogilvy saw no point in exchanging the confines of Edinburgh Castle for Tower Hill. Instead, they made their way by back roads whenever possible to Hull, where there was a ship waiting to take them on to Rotterdam. At last, Lady Ogilvy and her maid got on board the ship that was to take them to safety on the Continent.

But even this was not the end of her adventures. Yet again, a rumour sprang up that the gentleman who had boarded the ship was in fact Prince Charlie himself! A search party of soldiers was sent for and came onboard the ship. Luckily, Lady Ogilvy and her maid were aware of what was about to happen. So, when the soldiers appeared on the deck of the ship they were met by her maid. She told them that this was no prince but merely her mistress, who had fallen into debt and was heading abroad to avoid bringing her family into disgrace. When she opened the door of the cabin to show the beautiful Lady Ogilvy sitting at a table in a fancy gown, with her shoulders and upper bosom bare, none of the soldiers had any doubt that this was no man! She escaped to the Low Countries and headed to France where she was soon re-united with David.

This, though, was still not the end of Margaret's adventures. In 1751, she found out that she was carrying a child. She and David realised that if the son they were hoping for was to have any hope of ever succeeding to his grandfather's estates, it was imperative that he was born in Scotland. So, heavily pregnant, she returned to Scotland in disguise. In her own family's house at Auchter-house, not far from Dundee, she was delivered of her baby. To everyone's delight it was a boy, and a day later his birth was registered by the local minister. She knew that she could not remain in Scotland. If she did it would only be a matter of time before she was arrested and jailed, or worse! So, a few weeks later a tearful Lady Ogilvy took a farewell of her newborn son to return to France.

He was to be brought up by his grandparents and in time would succeed to the title and lands that were his due, but Lady Ogilvie realised that she would most likely never see her child again. And so it was, for she died at Boulogne in 1757 without setting eyes on her child or her native land again. As for the son she had risked liberty, and perhaps life, to have, her son born in her native land, he grew up severely mentally impaired and never did succeed his grandfather. Her last great adventure had been for nothing.

A friend's help

The Ogilvies were not the only leading family in Scotland to apparently hedge their bets in the Jacobite civil wars. When Prince Charles arrived in Scotland in 1745 it wasn't long before Donald Cameron of Locheil, chief of his clan, declared for the cause. His brother John, however, did not pledge his allegiance and had tried to dissuade his brother from taking the clan out in support of the Jacobite cause, but to no effect. When the Camerons marched south with the prince there was no sign of John. After the failure of the uprising, Locheil joined the prince onboard the *Heureux* when it sailed for France on 20 September 1746.

Due to John's refusal to go along with his brother, the house at Fassifern was spared by the British Army as it rampaged through the area, even though the prince had stayed there for a couple of nights. Like many of the great landholdings of the Highlands, the Cameron lands were put under Government control, and, as always, they needed someone to act as factor. John Cameron was the ideal candidate. Brother of the chief living in exile, he had no taint of Jacobitism about him, and he could hope to count on the loyalty of the local people. Now, the job of factor was one in which money could be made, but Government agents kept an eye out for possible dealings with the exiled Jacobites. This situation carried on until May 1753 when John was arrested on the charge of having corresponded with 'attainted persons', namely his brother. It seems there was suspicion that he might also have been sending him money raised on the estate by the tenants. John was arrested and carted off to Edinburgh, where he was imprisoned in the castle. He soon got bail though and returned. If he thought his troubles were over he was wrong, very wrong. He was soon rearrested and charged with a whole series of offences. He was suspected of having got some of the Loch Arkaig treasure – the gold that had been left behind by Charles Edward Stewart to bolster Jacobite support – and to hopefully keep the embers of rebellion from completely dying out. Furthermore, he was accused of having sold timber from the Locheil estates without the permission of the Government Trustees. Even more damning, though, was that he was also accused of having been involved in the murder of Colin Campbell of Glenure, the Red Fox, for whose death James of the Glens was to pay with his life. Yet again, he found himself locked up in Edinburgh Castle, but this time with a much more serious set of charges against him.

It was at this point that an old friend, Cumming of Achdalieu, came to visit him. Despite the recent troubles and the charges against him, it was still possible for John to receive visitors. Cumming had heard that John had been rearrested and had come to see if there was anything he could do to help. And there *was* something he could do for his friend.

'Well, it's kind you to visit,' said Fassifern, when his friend came into his cell, 'are you well?'

The two of them proceeded to chat lightly for a while till they were sure there was no one to overhear them. At that point their voices dropped to a low murmur as the two Highland gentlemen put their heads close together. Cameron spoke fast and Cumming listened intently. Time was of the essence. The Government agents were setting out soon for a visit to Fassifern and John knew if Cumming couldn't get there before them that he would be in a great deal of trouble. So Achdalieu left quickly and that same day was seen spurring his horse out of the city, heading north. Stopping only to rest his horse, grabbing what food he could and sleeping only in short bursts, he headed to Perth then through the mountains to Fort William and on to Fassifern on the northern shore of Loch Eil itself. He had driven himself to the point of exhaustion and was told by a trusted Cameron to whom John had directed him that Government agents were in the area. In fact, he was only minutes ahead of them by the time he got to the house. However, he knew exactly what he was doing and dismounted a hundred yards or so beyond the house to the west. He led his horse into the trees and hitched its reins to a branch. He then ran back and into the house and straight to Fassifern's study. There, he grabbed a small chest of papers and letters and climbed out of the window and disappeared into the woods behind the house. He had just made it into the trees when he heard a noise from the study. There, looking out of the open window, were two of the Government agents. They looked around suspiciously for a few seconds then closed the window and turned to join their colleagues behind them in the room. Breathing a sigh of relief, Cumming walked deeper into the woods and, using a trowel he had brought with him, he dug a hole. Into the hole went the chest, and the evidence that would have convicted John Cameron of Fassifern on at least two of the charges against him was gone. Filling in the hole, the exhausted Cumming moved carefully through the trees to where he had left his horse and, mounting it, headed back towards Fort William.

A few weeks later John Cameron was put on trial. The charge was that he had forged a deed that laid claim to the whole estate. The Government agents had found no evidence to support the charge, but on the earlier charge of corresponding with attainted persons he was found guilty. The Government had intercepted one of his letters and the case was unarguable. The judge,

however, showed some mercy – after all, he had been corresponding with his brother and there was nothing obviously incriminating in the letter. So the punishment was that of being banished for
ten years. Not banished from Great Britain but from Scotland! So
John Cameron spent the next ten years of his life at Alnwick, just
over the border in Northumberland, before returning to Fassifern.
Cumming's loyalty to his friend had saved John from a much
worse fate. In the final analysis, Cumming might not have fought
in the Jacobite army but the ties of blood and kin were far stronger
than any loyalty he might have felt to the House of Hanover.

A sad end

⟫◆⟪

Not all Jacobite prisoners were executed or sent as slaves to the plantations in the West Indies. Some of the lucky ones were simply locked up in Edinburgh Castle. One of these was Thomas Ogilvie from Eastmiln in Glenisla, who was out in the '45 serving as a captain in the regiment raised by his distant cousin David, Lord Ogilvy. After his regiment was disbanded at the head of Glenclova after Culloden he decided for some reason to head back home. Here, he thought he might be able to return to his old life, but there was little chance of that. The Government was intent on hunting down and capturing as many of what they considered Jacobite traitors as they could. The Hessian troops stationed at the Ogilvies' ancestral home, Cortachy Castle near the foot of Glen Clova, had the remit to scout the area for rebels, and it was only a matter of time before the commander heard that Thomas had returned home and came looking for him. Thomas was living openly at Eastmiln so it was a simple matter to arrest him and take him for trial to Edinburgh. Here, he was, as expected, found guilty of treason, and, no doubt because of his social standing, he was sentenced to be imprisoned in Edinburgh Castle, escaping both the executioner and the often worse fate of being transported to the West Indies, where so many Jacobites lived short miserable existences as slaves on the sugar plantations. Thomas was obviously considered a man of some standing for although many people were kept prisoner in the castle at various times, most of them were moved to other prisons after a short while. Among the more permanent guests, along with Thomas, were the Earl of Kellie, MacDonald of Kingsburgh, MacDonald of Glengarry, Lady Strathallan and the redoubtable Lady Ogilvy. Many prisoners were released under an Act of Indemnity in 1747, but Thomas was not released.

Perhaps, though, he simply was not well enough connected. While others had influential relatives working for their release, there was no way the Earl of Airlie could try and intervene, given the prominent role his son David had played in the rebellion. Thomas also had no real money of his own and was rationed, or fed by the Government, at the rate of a shilling a day. So the years passed and Thomas began to think that he would never see his beloved hills again. He decided that the only thing he could do was escape. Although the security at Edinburgh Castle had been little more than a joke before the '45, ever since the failed attempt to capture it things had been tightened up. However, Thomas was sure he could manage to get free and began to lay his plans. By May 1751, he had managed to get his hands on a net. He had found it lying on the battlements on one of the occasional walks the prisoners were allowed, and he reckoned it would give him a good chance of getting down from the castle walls to the rock on which the fortress stood. He was a man used to the mountains and was sure that once he was out on the cliff-face he could make his way safely down to the flat lands below the Castle Rock and then make off homewards. He did not think much beyond seeing his family and his beloved hills once more. He knew that it would not be easy, as he would have to make his escape in the hours of darkness and feel his way down the steep rock, but he was set on his plan of action. Even if he could only stay a short while in Glenisla before heading abroad into exile, he felt that anything would be better than carrying on as he was, cooped up in a cell in

Edinburgh Castle. He had long been able to get out of the cell in which he was kept at night and spent several weeks scouting for a suitable place to tie his net. At last he found what he was looking for, a stout iron ring set well in to the inner side of the battlements alongside one of the batteries of cannon on the north side. So, waiting till after dark on 21 May, he slipped out of his cell for the last time carrying the net he had been hiding. Checking that the guards were all elsewhere he made for the chosen point. Here, he tied the net firmly to the iron ring, threw it over the wall and, with a last look round the place he had been imprisoned for the previous five years, he clambered over the battlements and began to climb down Castle Rock.

In the morning, as first light came over the castle, one the guards noticed the net. At once he called for the officer of the watch and looked out over the wall. All he could see was the net blowing gently in the wind. It ended just more than half way down the wall of the castle. A party was sent out to look below, and there, at the foot of the cliff face below the castle, they found the crumpled body of Thomas Ogilvie. It appears that his skills as a mountaineer had done him no good for, the net being too short, he had had to drop in the dark on to the cliff face and had been unable to stop himself falling down the great rock face and fracturing his skull. He had escaped the confines of his prison cell only to fall to his death.

The good ship *Veteran*

—❖—

In the aftermath of Culloden the niceties of justice prevailed little in the courts set up to try the rebels. The House of Hanover had squashed the rebellion and was intent on punishing those who had dared to question their rule. Even the law itself was secondary to getting revenge, and there is perhaps some doubt as to the legality of trying Scottish prisoners in England given the existence of a separate Scots law. However, this was something that was unlikely to be brought up by any members of the Scottish Bar who understood well enough which side their bread was buttered. For the Jacobite prisoners, though, such points were of little concern – they had been captured and they would now be punished. The execution of notable figures like Kinlochmoidart and Tirnadris by being hung, drawn and quartered was truly barbaric, and many others were hanged, or simply died, in prison. Others again were sentenced to be transported to the West Indies to work in the sugar plantations there, which many thought a fate even worse than death. Transportation was not, in fact, an option that existed under Scots law, but as many of the rebels were tried in England such niceties could be ignored. The Jacobites who were sent out to Jamaica and other islands were effectively slaves, and many of them died of disease in the tropical conditions.

One of the ships that transported Jacobite prisoners was the *Veteran*, under the command of Captain Ricky. The ship was hired by the contractor Samuel Smith and left Liverpool for the island of Antigua on 8 May 1747. On board were 150 Jacobite prisoners, gathered from the jails in Carlisle, Lincoln and York. Many of them were in a pitiful condition after nearly a year in captivity. They came from all over Scotland – Highland and Lowland, east and west – and some were from the North of England. There were even a few Campbells from Argyll, showing that not all of that clan were staunch Hanoverians. Many of the prisoners were in their teens, and it is interesting that the majority of those from the Highland areas, like Patrick Grant from Badenoch and Duncan McPherson from Inverness, were listed on the ship's manifest as labourers. Some of them were even younger, like Peter Sumerall from Angus who, at thirteen, had served as drummer boy in Lord Ogilvy's regiment. Fifteen of the one hundred and fifty prisoners were women, and, though all Scottish born, came, like the men, from both Highland and Lowland areas. Amongst the contingent of prisoners were weavers, herdsmen, shoemakers and tailors. There was also a goldsmith, a watchmaker, a bookbinder and a couple of gentlemen, in the parlance of the time. This, combined with the geographic spread of the prisoners' birthplaces, reflects the fact that support for the Stewarts was spread throughout all walks of life in most areas of the British Isles. The '45 was truly a civil war.

One can imagine what conditions were like on board ship and that many of the prisoners, who had never been on board a ship before, would have been badly affected by seasickness. This, combined with their removal from everything they knew, their futures mapped out for them as plantation slaves in all but name, would have ensured that they had a miserable time. However, things were about to change.

On the 28 June they were approaching the island of Antigua, where the prisoners were to be disembarked, when the ship's lookout spotted sails on the horizon. The other ship came towards the *Veteran*, and soon it was obvious that it was a French warship. It was the cruiser *Diamond*, out of Martinique. Peter Sumerall and a couple of the other youngest lads had been let out of their shackles and allowed up from the hold for a short while to help with scrubbing the decks. He was knocked down as Captain Ricky sent his men up the ratlines to pile on as much sail as they could. Being at war with France and well aware that his ship was fair game for the *Diamond*, Ricky intended to try and outrun her. As the sailors climbed aloft, Peter Sumerall and the other lads were slapped around the head and thrown back down below decks.

As the ship heeled and surged under the increased sails above, he was bombarded with questions: 'What's happening above?', 'What's going on?', 'Did you see anything, lad?' The questions came thick and fast, some of them in the strange language the Highlanders spoke that he did not understand a word of.

'All right, all right,' shouted Peter, 'let me speak. There's a big ship coming towards us and I heard the lookout shout that she was a Frenchie.'

'A Frenchman,' someone said, 'maybe we'll be captured.'

'Will they set us free?' said another voice. Yet another asked, 'Will she fire on us?', a question that brought silence for a second or two. Then there was a hubbub of voices as what was being said was translated for those who only spoke Gaelic. Within minutes people were all talking animatedly to their neighbours. Whatever was to happen now, the dreadful mind-numbing boredom and despair of the previous month had lifted from them.

Up above, Captain Ricky was watching the approaching cruiser through his telescope. He soon realised there was no way he could hope to outrun her. Although the *Veteran* carried a handful of cannon, there was no way he could fight her off and he knew he would have to surrender. Soon the *Diamond* was close enough to fire a warning shot across the bows of the *Veteran*, and Ricky reluctantly gave the order to shorten sail and strike the colours on her topmast. Within a few minutes a couple of boatloads of French sailors had come aboard, and, under the orders of a French officer, the ship veered off from its course to Antigua and headed to Martinique.

One of the prisoners, John Ostler, a gentleman from Lincolnshire, spoke to the French officer who came below decks and, after a few minutes conversation, addressed the entire hold full of shackled prisoners.

'Listen everyone,' he said, realising that every pair of eyes in the gloom was fixed on him. 'This gentleman has said he will have us out of irons as soon as he can. We are sailing to Martinique and we are to be set free.'

A cacophony of cheering erupted. Many of them hadn't dared to hope for such a release. But the impossible had happened. They were not going to be slaves after all.

Within a short while the prisoners were unshackled and, in small groups, were allowed up on deck. For the majority of them this was the first fresh air they had breathed since being herded at gunpoint into the filthy hold of the ship all those weeks earlier. A couple of days later they found themselves on dry land, on the French island of Martinique, free.

The capture of the *Veteran* was soon reported back in Britain. Sam Smith, who had contracted to send the prisoners out to Antigua, was furious. The French action had cost him money. So he approached the Duke of Newcastle, a member of the Privy Council, to ask for a letter to be sent to Governor Matthews of the Leeward Islands demanding the handover of the prisoners. It was January 1748 before Matthews managed to get an agent to take a letter to Charles de Tubieres, the Marquis de Caylus, asking for the prisoners to be handed over. This Caylus was not prepared to do without explicit instructions from France, something he was aware he was extremely unlikely to receive. By now, of course, the prisoners had dispersed. Smith refused to give up and went again to the Privy Council, this time asking that 'when any sea cartel or exchange of prisoners is to be agreed on with France, these rebel prisoners now at Martinique may be included specially in such a cartel, to be delivered to his agent, Mr John Chalmers, in Antigua'. The French Government were hardly likely to heed any request from the British Privy Council so Sam Smith lost his profit.

As for the prisoners, little is known of what happened to them, other than that several, including Daniel Ross from Ross-shire, John Kennedy from Perth and the drummer, Peter Sumerall, from Angus, managed to make their way to the British colonies in North America, where they and their descendants probably took great pleasure in fighting against the British Government thirty years later in the American War of Independence.

THE LIGHTER SIDE

The white cockade

Cockades were decorative ribbons affixed to hats, and the Jacobites of the '45 adopted white ones as a sign of their loyalty to the Stewart cause. Given that most of the Jacobite Army were irregular troops, and that uniforms were a rarity, they served as a useful identification, in battle as well as on the streets of Scotland's towns, once the campaign was underway. There have been those who have said that the reason the white cockade was chosen was because Prince Charlie picked a white rose and stuck it in his own bonnet, a story that is thought to have inspired the Robert Burns song 'My Love was born in Aberdeen'. However, as different-coloured cockades or hat decorations had been used as a sign of political and military allegiances since the seventeenth century this is hardly likely. It is an example of the kind of story, and song, that came into being in the late eighteenth and early nineteenth centuries, as the horrors of Culloden faded from public consciousness and the fear of resurgent Jacobitism was overtaken by a romantic view of Scotland's past, popularised by Sir Walter Scott and others. That said, chivalry was not unknown amongst the Jacobites.

During the sojourn of the Highland army in England in November 1745, a party of MacDonalds approached Rose Castle near Carlisle, which was then occupied by a man called Dacre, from Cumberland. The Highlanders came to the castle doors, fully armed, and demanded to be quartered there in such a way as to make it clear that they had no intention of being refused. The butler, or servant, who answered the door was no coward and refused to be intimated.

'I'm afraid, Sir,' he said calmly to Donald MacDonald of Kinlochmoidart, who was leading the contingent, 'that it is a most inconvenient time.'

'Whatever do you mean?' demanded MacDonald, a bit taken aback at the man's coolness and bravery.

'Well, Sir, the lady of the house, Mrs Dacre, has just given birth to a fine young daughter, and, as you can imagine, we are all at sixes and sevens,' the man replied.

'God forbid that I or any of my kin here should give the lady any further inconvenience at such a time,' MacDonald said and, turning to his companions, he addressed them briefly in Gaelic.

Most of the contingent turned as if to go when a thought crossed MacDonald's mind. Perhaps this was just a clever ploy. Calling to his kinsmen to wait for a few minutes, he turned back to the man standing at the castle door.

'Would you think it possible that your mistress would let me see the infant,' he asked in a polite but decisive manner. The servant was left in no doubt that this was no request but an order, and, given the presence of so many heavily armed Highlanders, an order that would have to be obeyed.

'I can see no harm in that at all,' said the servant, as calm as you like. 'If you will just wait here a minute, Sir, I shall see if I can fetch the child.'

He turned and went back inside only to reappear a few minutes later accompanied by a young maid, who was carrying the new-born infant warmly wrapped in a blanket. She brought the infant to Kinlochmoidart and held her up for him to see.

Looking down on the infant with a smile, the fierce-looking Highland warrior took his bonnet from his head. Then, unpinning the white cockade from the bonnet he pinned it to the front of the blanket the newborn babe was wrapped in.

'There,' he said with a gentle smile. 'That will be a token to any of our comrades who come this way that Donald MacDonald of Kinlochmoidart has taken the family of Castle Rose under his protection.'

He then turned to the servant and, looking beyond him into the castle itself, saw a man standing in the shadows beyond the door. He called for the man to come forward. It was the child's father and, after congratulating him on the birth of his daughter, Donald shook the clearly terrified man by the hand and said, 'You will not be bothered further by any of our troops and may the child be healthy and happy all her days.'

He then turned and said a few more words to his men at which point the entire contingent departed.

As for the white cockade, it became a treasured possession in the Dacre family and was particularly appreciated by Mary Dacre, who was the baby brought to the door. Throughout her childhood she repeatedly asked to be told the story of what had happened when the Highlanders arrived on the day of her birth. When she grew up she married and became Lady Clerk of Penicuik, and every year on her birthday she took great pleasure in wearing the white cockade in remembrance of the gallant Highland chief who had called at Rose Castle in 1745.

As for Donald, he paid the ultimate price for his loyalty to the Jacobite cause.

A Jacobite blackbird

⟫◈⟪

In the years between the risings of 1715 and 1745 there was a great deal of Jacobite plotting going on. Though much of it, no doubt, consisted of little more than bravado in taverns, all the while more serious plans were being laid. One of the most common manifestations of support for the Jacobite cause was the surreptitious toast to the 'king over the water'. This could be accomplished in the midst of a normal conversation simply by passing the right hand over one's glass, a simple sign understood by all true Jacobite supporters and many of those who simply played at it. For, amongst the less privileged ranks of contemporary society, as has been the case in many human societies at many times, there was a strong tendency to support anyone other than whoever was currently in power, particularly if there was some chance those currently holding power would be humbled. These sentiments were made worse in Scotland by the resentment that had been caused by the bribery and corruption that had led to the Treaty of Union in 1707.

Such Jacobite and anti-Government attitudes greatly distressed some of the more devout Protestants in the capital, who were fiercely opposed to the return of the Stewart dynasty. Some were very much in the habit of following the tenets of their Covenanting forebears, one of which was a strict adherence to Sabbatarianism, the idea that the only acceptable activities people could participate in on Sundays were those that involved contemplation and prayer.

A group of them lived together in the closes around the West Bow in the 1730s. Such was their excessive piety that they were known to the rest of the city's population as the Bowhead Saints.

As is usually the case with over pious people, they were not known for their sense of humour and believed that everyone should do as they did. Even well into the eighteenth century there were still citizens' patrols that walked the streets during divine service on a Sunday on the lookout for those who they considered to be breaking the Sabbath. Wise folk simply kept out of sight during the various hours of a Sunday that these patrols were about. Some of their actions were the subject of local gossip, like the time when they came upon a joint of meat roasting over an open fire in the back vennel of one of the closes. Such blatant Sabbath-breaking was not to be tolerated, and the patrol duly confiscated the meat from off its spit leaving its owner and his family hungry. However, as they themselves had had no hand in its cooking, it was deemed permissible for them to see the provision of this succulent feast as divine providence and they had no hesitation in devouring it themselves. Such were the practicalities of their idea of Christian commitment.

However, on another occasion they actually took a prisoner, one that, truth be told, caused them some problems. It was the custom amongst many people of the time to buy songbirds and teach them to pipe the tunes of the current songs of their own party, Jacobite or Whig. One Saturday evening a staunch Jacobite had left his blackbird in its cage outside a window in his tenement close in the West Bow, possibly because he was more concerned with singing songs himself as result of having had a glass or two of claret in a nearby tavern. Rolling home after dark he forget all about his bird in its cage. Anyway, come the morning the bird happily began trilling away its limited repertoire of tunes, all of which were anti-Hanoverian. Its owner lay in his bed oblivious of what was going on as the hour of the first Sunday service approached. Never a devout man, he was unconcerned that he might miss going to church. And so it came to pass that the devout band of brothers scouring the streets for sinners came past his window. To their shock and horror, as they approached they heard the bird giving forth the scandalous and treasonous tune, 'The King Shall Come Into His Own Again'. The place where its cage was attached to the wall could be accessed from several different apartments, and they were at a loss as to who should carry the blame for this disgraceful affair.

As always with such groups, there was one person who felt the affront so badly he felt he must do something. Accordingly, he got his companions to fetch a ladder, up which he climbed and removed the bird in its cage from the wall. Coming down with the bird, he looked at his companions, all of whom were a little quizzical as to what he intended doing now. But such men are always ready to rise to any occasion, and he said, with something of an air of solemnity, 'Right, we shall just lock this foul creature up in the guardroom.'

Whether he hoped a spell in the clink would make the bird mend its ways is unclear. The man's pomposity gave rise to some verses by Pennycook, a local rhymester, who put these words in the poor man's mouth:

> Had ye been taught by me, a Bowhead Saint,
> You'd sung the Solemn League and Covenant,
> Bessy of Lanark, or the Last Good-Night,
> But you're a bird prelatic – that's not right.
> Oh, could my baton reach those laverock too;
> They're chanting Jamie, Jamie, just like you.
> I hate vain birds lead malignant lives,
> But love the chanters to the Bowhead wives.

This soon became popular in those taverns where the silent toast to the King over the Water was common, and many were taken by the notion that even the larks were singing of the return of the Stewarts. What the Bowhead Saints said when confronted with the lines, as they must have been, has not come down to us.

Ye'll tak a dram

'Ye'll tak a dram?' is a question that truly reflects the history of Scottish hospitality. The phrase, in Scots, one of Scotland's two indigenous languages, although phrased as a question, really means – you will have a drink! Though the term dram generally refers to whisky these days, it can, in fact, be used of any spirit.

After fleeing from Culloden, Prince Charlie was approaching the River Lochy with a small group of companions, which included Lochiel, Chief of the Clan Cameron, who had been the dominant power in the area since time immemorial. The river was rather high and all of the boats in the immediate area had been burnt by Government troops, who were combing the area looking for Prince Charlie. They were met at the riverside by Clunes Cameron, who told them he had an old boat hidden that had been carried over from Loch Arkaig. When he saw the boat, Lochiel was a bit concerned. It was old and cracked and to his eyes looked totally unsafe. He was reluctant to entrust either his own or the prince's safety to such a craft. When he said this to Clunes, the latter replied, 'I shall cross first and show you the way.'

Locheil agreed to this and Clunes asked him, 'Will you take a dram then?'

'Och aye, what do you have?' replied the chief.

'Well, I have half a dozen bottles of brandy that were liberated from the Redcoats, and I think in this weather both you and the prince would be the better of a dram or two,' came the reply.

The prince was delighted, not only with the thought of a warming nip but with the idea that it had been provided by his enemies. It was small recompense for the dreadful defeat he had suffered, but it cheered him up a little. So a toast or two was made and within a few minutes three of the bottles were finished off. So, with the group fortified by brandy, the boat crossed the river three times, rowed by a couple of Lochiel's Cameron clansmen. First, Cluny went with three of the company. Then, Lochiel crossed with the same number, and, finally, the prince himself went, with two further companions. However, by the third crossing the old boat was showing its age: it was leaking like a sieve and the bottom was awash with water. In the efforts to bail and to cross the river as quickly as possible the remaining three bottles of brandy were broken. However, everyone got across safely, and once the prince was safe on shore he called for another dram.

'I am afraid that is impossible, Your Majesty,' said Clunes ruefully, 'the last three bottles were broken in the crossing.'

This, however, was no obstacle to the two Camerons who had been rowing the boat: they simply treated the contents of the bottom of the boat as a form of punch and proceeded to drink the lot. The result was that they were so 'fleein' that they kept the rest of the company amused for hours afterward on their journey westwards.

Bareback riding

⋙◆⋘

In the years after Culloden the English troops garrisoned throughout the Highlands were prone to what we now know as depression. Modern ideas of tourism and of the beauty of the rugged mountains were still some way ahead, and many of the soldiers found the soaring rock faces, dark forests and tumbling streams unpleasant and disturbing. In addition, most of them were, to all intents and purposes, living in a foreign land as well as an alien landscape. Most of them would have come from England's teeming cities or the well-ordered countryside of large farms and substantial villages. In the Highlands there was little other than small groups of *tigh dubh*, or black houses, the simple dwellings of the Highland people, in which animals and humans occupied the same building, which was permanently filled with peat smoke. The fact that the subsistence economy of the Highlands, and the efficiency of the black houses in countering the often harsh weather, spoke of a society well adjusted to its physical environment would have escaped them. To most of them, the Highlanders, with their strange garb and even stranger language, would have seemed little more than savages, an opinion encouraged by both the army and the Government. When you add the fact that they knew that the local population were giving secret support to the guerrilla campaign of those rebels who had 'stayed out', living by the age-old traditions of cattle raiding, and with whom they could be called on to fight at any time, it's easy to understand that there was often a bit of a morale problem amongst the troops.

The biggest garrison was at Fort Augustus on the southern shore of Loch Ness, and in the summer of 1746 the Duke of Cumberland, the son of King George III, was in residence at the fort. Numerous stories have been told of murder, rapes, arson and other crimes carried out against the unfortunate local people by English soldiers from the garrison, all with the apparent approval of Cumberland. As far as he was concerned, the Highlanders were rebels and savages and hardly even human. The widespread looting and destruction meant that the local population were living in desperate circumstances, many of them on the verge of starvation. In the harsh winter of that year many did starve to death. Cumberland imposed severe penalties on any who offered even a crust of bread to the starving and defeated Highlanders.

Within the fort, life was relatively good as there was plenty to eat and drink, but there was still the problem of low morale. In June, even as the ravaging of Highland Scotland continued, Cumberland came up with an idea to entertain his troops, many of whom were English and Hessians from Germany, with a considerable number of 'loyal' Lowland and Highland Scots among them. He decided to organise a series of horse races for the troops. This was not to be a race between the highly trained dragoons on their great powerful steeds, it was to be a race for the infantry, riding on the local garrons, or Highland ponies. A great deal of drink was laid on for the day, and prizes were offered for the winners. An added wrinkle, intended to make things as entertaining as possible, was that the riders were not allowed saddles: they had to ride bareback.

A combination of the free-flowing drink, widespread betting

and the antics of the riders, many of whom had never sat on a horse before, provided a great deal of enjoyment for the gathered troops and their camp-followers. In those far off times it was normal for wives to accompany soldiers on campaign, to cook for them, tend their wounds when necessary and generally provide all kinds of essential backup.

Such was the popularity of the first series of races that one of the officers suggested to Cumberland that a prize should be put up for a race between soldiers' wives. In those days it was still the norm for ladies to ride horses side-saddle, but, as one of the officers was heard to remark, 'These women ain't ladies.' The women's race aroused even greater merriment than the men's races because they rode the Highland ponies bareback like their husbands and, just like their husbands, sat astride them. Unlike their husbands, however, there was an extra aspect to the ladies' bareback riding. Not only were they riding astride the bareback horses, in order to give as much entertainment as possible to the assembled drunken soldiery, they too were bare backed! It seems that the duke himself was present, and no doubt he had a grand old time watching the naked ladies racing flat-out on the wee Highland ponies, behaviour that would have been considered unacceptable amongst the so-called uncivilised Highlanders. The prize, which was a fine smock, was won by the wife of one of the soldiers from the Old Buffs regiment.

The jollity of the day was further enhanced by a series of footraces amongst the soldiers; again, extensive drinking and betting intensified the fun. Even the officers joined in, and General Hawley, perhaps best remembered for his gallant flight from Falkirk, managed to beat Colonel Howard by a nose, both of them also riding shelties or garrons. So, as the people of the Highlands suffered their crops being destroyed, their cattle and other stock being 'appropriated' and their houses being burned-down by troops who could loot, rape and kill with impunity, the British Army were rewarded with a grand day out at Fort Augustus, laid on by their commander-in-chief, the Duke of Cumberland.

General Wade
and Patrick Grant

In July 1724 General George Wade was given the job of writing a report on the situation in the Highlands by the king, George II. For centuries Scottish and British governments had been susceptible to attack from the Highlands. Given the nature of these attacks, which utilised the fighting and raiding skills of the armed clansmen, governments generally found themselves at a disadvantage in that the Highlanders, if they thought themselves threatened, would simply retreat into the mountains and disperse, leaving any troops who followed then chasing shadows. Here, they could carry on guerrilla-type campaigns, just as their ancestors had been doing since the Romans had marched into the country nearly two millennia earlier. Once they were back in the Highlands they were difficult to dislodge, and moving large bodies of men was, at the least, extremely difficult.

Once the report was submitted, George II immediately appointed Wade Commander-in-Chief, North Britain, and the general began to organise garrisons of Government troops in the Highlands. His plan was specifically to be able to mobilise soldiers to move at short notice throughout the Highlands, quelling disturbances, disarming clans where necessary, and forming allegiances with clans loyal to the House of Hanover as he went. This all depended on creating a network of roads through the

Highlands, a network which has become known as General Wade's roads. There has long been a misconception that the roads were built after the '45 to open up the Highlands, but they had been under construction since two decades earlier. Many were later upgraded to become our modern highways, but in many parts of the country the old military roads can still be clearly seen; the construction methods of eighteenth-century road building meant they had to follow the contours of the landscape more than in more modern times. Some of these roads followed what had been traditional cattle-droving trails, trails that had been used for centuries by the cateran or cattle-raiders, whom the Government were keen to stamp out. Apart from allowing the swift movement of troops and much better communications, it was an added advantage from the Government's point of view that the very existence of the roads was a means of weakening the essentially subsistence economy of the Highlands that the clan system was founded on. With the introduction of new communications and the money economy the old patterns of clan life came under attack from forces that, if not so obvious as the introduction of numerous garrisons of red-coated troops, were, in effect, much more profound and long-lasting. No longer would the inaccessibility of the Scottish Highlands serve as a bulwark against the changing social and economic patterns of the rest of the country.

By summer 1725 the first military road was being built. Three years later, while pushing the road through Strathspey, Wade made the acquaintance of Patrick Grant of Rothiemurchus, whose hospitality and conviviality were well known. It was the custom for all Highlanders, and especially clan chiefs and other men of substance, to be hospitable. In fact, it was a fundamental part of Highland society that hospitality had to be offered to passers-by if asked for. In those days there were few inns and people made their own whisky. Communal entertainment, the ceilidh, would generally take place in people's houses or barns. Grant, a man of some standing in the community, was known to be well off and really knew how to push the boat out. Wade, like most soldiers, was fond of eating and, of course, drinking and was so pleased with the treatment he got at Rothiemurchus that he returned again and again. Being a general he, of course, could not travel alone, so Grant had the additional burden of feeding and looking after whichever aides and attachés Wade brought with him.

Now Grant was a Loyalist and had no sympathy for the Jacobite cause, believing that it had no real chance of success. He considered himself to be a forward-thinking person and thought that the restitution of the Stewarts would be a backward step for the country. However, his loyalty had limits and it wasn't too long before he was getting rather fed up of Wade's visits. The general was a pleasant enough companion but enough was enough, and it seemed that the Englishman was taking advantage of his hospitality by being such a frequent visitor. Road-building, then as now, was a slow process, and Grant realised that Wade could be coming to him month after month if he did not do something about it. So, he decided on a course of action he was sure would bring him the result he wanted. It had become the custom for them after dinner to retire to the study, just the pair of them, for a few glasses of brandy and one night Grant, after making sure that everyone else in the house was in bed, brought the situation to a head.

He locked the door of the room they were in, pocketed the key, sat down and proceded to pour a couple of large glasses of brandy. The general was reaching for his glass when he raised his head and found himself looking down the barrel of a clearly loaded and cocked pistol.

'Good God, Grant,' he spluttered, 'what do you think you are doing man?'

'Well, General,' said his host with hard smile, 'I want you to join me in a toast. I think our friendship can stand this toast, I am just being a trifle cautious.'

Then he stood up, took his glass in his left hand and in a loud voice said 'The King', passing the glass of brandy over the decanter of water on the table in front of him, his right hand still holding the pistol. This was, of course, the Jacobite toast, 'the King over the Water', to the man the Jacobites thought of as James the VIII and III. Wade went white, rose to his feet and went to the door, saying not a word. Still holding the pistol, Grant unlocked the door and let the general leave. By the time he rose in the morning there was no sign of Wade, who had risen at dawn and left with his companions. Never again did he feel free to visit Grant of Rothiemurchius. Nor did he try to do anything about this blatant disloyalty to the Hanoverian crown. Perhaps the good general thought it might raise a question or two as to what he was doing regularly drinking with a man who held such ideas.

How not to capture a castle

⟫•◆•⟪

In eighteenth-century Scotland people liked a drink. In fact, they liked more than one and some of the reports of the time of how much people drank are little short of frightening. All walks of society, from labourers to High Court Judges, were liable to start the day with a glass of ale or wine and the taking of a 'meridian' before noon was normal. Drink was taken with all meals and, particularly in the capital, people spent their evenings in taverns and clubs. Water supplies in the eighteenth century were none too clean and, where nowadays we might drink tea or coffee, back then alcohol in one form or another was the norm. The keyword was conviviality and all levels of business, trade, politics and even legal meetings took place in licensed premises. It was not an uncommon sight for even the loftiest of politicians or judges to be carried home after the curfew was called at ten o'clock. Most of those who could afford it drank claret imported from France, a trade that provided a handy cover for Jacobite communications for nearly a century. It wasn't just men who drank either. Women, too, liked a drink and some of the contemporary reports make it seem as if Edinburgh in the middle of the eighteenth century was a city floating on a tide of alcohol. While there were undoubted casualties – and both Robert Fergusson and Robert Burns seemed to have paid the price of trying to keep up with the drinking scene in Edinburgh – drunkenness was in no way frowned upon. This might go some way to explaining one of the dafter incidents of the '45.

How not to capture a castle

Plans had been laid to make a surprise attack on Edinburgh Castle, without doubt the most high-profile Government establishment in Scotland. As well as being a dramatic strategic move it would also be a major propaganda coup. The castle contained a great deal of arms and ammunition as well as a large sum of money, in gold. This was the residue of the 'Equivalent', the money that had been sent to Scotland from England after the Union of 1707 as a means of helping equalise the burden of taxation in the two countries. Plans were laid locally and the date was set. Ensign Thomas Arthur, who was serving in the castle garrison, was one of the conspirators. On 6 September he approached one of the soldiers, James Thomson, who was on sentinel duty at the castle, and asked if they could meet up the following day at Thomas's house in the Canongate after Thomson came off duty. The ensign also approached another of the sentinels, John Holland, and sent him to bring Thomson to his house at two o'clock that afternoon. On their way there they met Thomas, who directed them to a nearby house where he told them to wait for him. This they did, and a short while later they were joined by the young officer, who asked to speak to Thomson alone. He then told him of the plan to take the castle, asked for his help and gave him forty shillings, telling him to come again the following day to a house in Weir's Land and this time to bring William Ainslie, another of the sentinels, with him. This he did, and on getting to the house they met Arthur and some other men, including Charles Forbes of Brux in Aberdeenshire, and a local Catholic man called Pringle, whose house it was. Forbes was said to have been recently with the king in exile. The upshot of all this was that Thomson and Ainslie were promised a hundred guineas and commissions as lieutenants in the Jacobite army for their cooperation in the attack.

The plan was that when the two sentinels were on duty that

night at nine o'clock they would hear a signal, at which point they were to let down a weighted rope from the castle ramparts. Corporal Holland was to be the lookout. The rope would then be attached to a ladder, which they would pull up. The assailants would then climb up the ladder and, with the advantage of the darkness and the element of surprise, would be able to disarm the guard and take the castle. As there were less than a hundred men in the castle and they were notoriously badly equipped the conspirators expected the affair to be over quickly. Once they had scaled the ramparts and got into the castle they would simply round up all the weapons and corner the majority of the soldiers in their beds. They would then either lock them in their sleeping quarters or march them down to the cells and put them behind bars. There would be no more than a handful of other sentries to be dealt with, and with the help of the three soldiers they did not expect any difficulties. They would then fire several of the castle cannon to let their friends know they had been successful and Jacobite troops would come to fully man the castle. There was also a plan for guns to be fired in series across the country to the north to let the Earl of Mar, up in Aberdeenshire, know of the success of the episode. Taking the weighted rope, which Thomson hid below his tunic, and receiving some of the promised money in advance, the two soldiers went to a nearby tavern for a drink then returned to their duties at the castle.

The day before this Ensign Arthur had told his brother, a doctor in the capital, what was about to happen. He was not a man able to keep a secret, and when asked by his wife what was bothering him he told her of the plan. She was anything but a Jacobite and soon sent off an anonymous warning to the Lord Justice Clerk, Sir Adam Cockburn of Ormiston. Now, Edinburgh had been awash with rumours of Jacobite attacks for weeks at the time, and when the governor of the castle, Lieutenant-colonel

Stuart, was informed of the planned attack he did nothing more than double the guard at the castle gate before going off to his bed. In truth, as it turned out, he had very little to worry about.

Nine o'clock came and went and Thomson and Ainslie heard and saw nothing. A full two hours after the allotted time Thomson heard a noise from the rock below.

'Who goes there?' he whispered, leaning over the rampart.

'It is Ensign Arthur,' came the reply. 'We are not quite ready yet, but drop the cord down, there's a good lad. Wait a while.'

Thomson was already in a state of some anxiety, having been waiting for two hours, but what made it worse was that he could clearly hear that Arthur had had a lot to drink. His words were slurred and Thomson suspected that Arthur and his companions had been in some nearby tavern 'powdering their hair' as the current slang put it. This was, in fact, the case; they had been celebrating the success of deed not yet done, and true to the spirit of the times they had not restrained themselves to one or two glasses! All the while that Thomson and Airlie had been sweating on the castle ramparts their co-conspirators had been drinking toasts to the king over the water.

After a short while a tug came on the rope. This was the signal to hoist the ladder. Ainslie and Thomson had only been pulling the ladder for a couple of minutes before Holland came running up.

'Quick, lads. Let it drop. Lieutenant Lindsay is coming on his rounds.'

At once, they let go of the ladder, which clattered down the rock, and shouts came from below as it fell among the men there. Lindsay came running.

'What is going on here, men?' he demanded, a drawn pistol in his hand.

'There is someone on the rock,' replied Ainslie.

'Right,' commanded the officer, 'fire at any sound you hear.'

All three levelled their guns down into the darkness and, as a couple of shouts came up, Holland fired into the darkness below. At once the alarm was sounded and the garrison jumped from their beds. Lindsay sent men out of the castle gate and round the rock with guns at the ready, some of them carrying torches. Reaching the point below where Lindsay, Ainslie, Holland and Thomson were standing, holding torches, they found two men, both the worse for drink. One was a Catholic priest and the other a stable lad called Graham who had been drawn into the plot. At this point a party of the town-guard, whom the Lord Provost had sent to patrol about the castle at the request of the Lord-Justice-Clerk, came up from the West Port. They had heard the shot and came running, but the event was already over.

Both the men were immediately arrested and carried off to the Tolbooth. There was no sign of the rest of the would-be attackers. In the morning it was also realised that the ladders that had been brought were far too short for their intended purpose! A second group of the plotters had just arrived at the foot of Castle Rock with more ladders when they heard Holland's shot and the rousing of the garrison. They dropped their ladders and ropes and fled into the night. Before nightfall that day a contingent of sixty well-armed troops were sent from Lord Islay, the Duke of Argyll's brother, to reinforce the castle garrison.

Once the affair had been fully investigated, Ainslie, Thomson and Holland were all tried and found guilty of a raft of charges. Ainslie was hanged on a gallows erected on the exact spot where the conspirators had intended climbing the wall. His body was left to swing in the breeze, hanging over the battlements for several weeks. His companions, Thomson and Holland, were surprisingly not hanged, but flogged, though that particular form of punishment was truly horrendous. Apart from the stable lad and the Catholic priest the rest of the conspirators had fled Edinburgh. While there is little doubt that the Government were lucky that the attempted seizure of the castle did not happen, we can only look back and wonder at the utter stupidity and carelessness of the men selected by Lord Drummond on behalf of his exiled king to attack the most important fortress in Scotland.

The main chance:
the story of John Coutts

———⊰◆⊱———

Now, John Coutts, from Woodend in Glenisla in the southern Grampians, was a man who was well known for being quick-witted and intelligent. But it seems he might not have been over-blessed in the way of morality and his neighbours would have told you that he was always on the lookout for the main chance. He was ready to turn his hand to anything profitable whenever the opportunity arose. In the eighteenth century the ancient clan traditions of cattle raiding had still not entirely died out, and there is no doubt that what Lowlanders might have seen as rampant criminality was thought of by Highlanders as not just suitable but in fact proper behaviour for a Highland gentleman. And as all men in the clan considered themselves to be relations of their chief, which most of them were, and as he was undoubtedly a gentleman, it must follow that they too had the same standing.

This could cause confusion with their Lowland cousins, parti-cularly after 1707 when the gradations in Lowland society be-came ever more rigid. In those places where the Lowlands and the Highlands adjoined, there were those who saw the areas where the differing traditions and outlooks of the Gaelic-speaking High-landers and the Scots-speaking Lowlanders overlapped as fertile ground for profit. John was one of these, but such was his sharpness of mind that he was never actually caught doing anything that could lead to criminal charges being brought against him.

When the '45 came along he, like many another Highlanders, saw an opportunity to gather a bit of personal wealth while serving in the Jacobite army. Certainly at first, it seems that he really had no opinion at all as regards the relative merits of the Stewart and Hanoverian claims to the throne. He simply thought that there was profit to be made in those uncertain times. Given the ages-old tradition of raiding amongst the clans he was hardly alone in that! So, he went out with the Jacobites in the hope of personal enrichment and, up till Culloden at least, he thought he was doing well enough. After that fateful battle and the subsequent disbanding of the last of the Jacobite forces at Ruthven, he returned to the Glenisla district. By now, mainly as a result of the slaughter on Drumossie Moor, his opinions had hardened and he was fervently anti-Hanoverian. It was well known that he had been out, and as the Government troops tightened their hold on the Highlands he became a fugitive. The Redcoats were scouring the area for rebels and he was forced to hide out in the hills. Like most of his kind he knew the hills well and could keep well out of reach of the red-coated soldiers. From the same hills he could see the widespread destruction that was taking place in the glens below.

One day, he saw a man being chased through one of the lesser glens off Glenisla by a bunch of red-coated soldiers. As the man approached him Johnnie whistled from behind a large boulder and, without letting the troops catch sight of him, waved the man over to where he was. He then offered to exchange clothes with the man and lead the troops off. The fugitive, who was breathing hard, agreed at once, and in a matter of moments they had swapped their clothes and Johnnie had taken off through the hills. His companion lay hidden in the heather as the troops streamed past. Now, Johnnie had been wandering all over the area since he was a bairn and it wasn't long before he gave the troops the slip. Once a reasonable time had passed he returned to where he had left the other man. He turned out to be James Carnegie of Balnamoon, who lived for many subsequent years in a cave in Glen Mark north of Brechin, and he swore that if he could ever do Johnnie a good turn he would only need to be asked.

Now, Johnnie was too well known in the area for there to be any chance of his being able to slip back into anything like a normal life, and he was soon out with a band of caterans, who, like the famous Serjeant Mor and his men, raided far and wide through central and northern Scotland. It didn't take long for his natural wit and intelligence to give him command over his companions. His planning was always excellent, and under his leadership the band lived well. Often, they were happy to raid the homes of Presbyterian ministers, most of whom were strong supporters of the Hanoverian cause and very anti-Jacobite. This made the ministers fair game in the eyes of Johnnie, and others who lived the outlaw life, the great majority of whom were of course Catholics and Episcopalians. The raiders were also happy, whenever the possibility arose, to revert to the more traditional target of cattle and other livestock. For many years such bands survived in the Highlands, but it was through their raiding of ministers that they slowly began to lose the support amongst the local populations that they needed to avoid the army patrols.

Sometimes, Johnnie's band of outlaws would pass through Glenisla, but Johnnie had no intention of raiding his own people and on more than one occasion had been known to come to a farm, wave to someone and stand by a dry-stane dyke. When the person who had been waved to got near they would hear Johnnie

Coutts say, 'I daurna say tae oniebodie but I'm tellin this dyke that there'll likely be an attempt made tae lift cattle here the morn's nicht.' So, forewarned, the people of Glenisla were spared the depredations of Coutt's band of caterans.

Courage to the end:
Simon Lovat's capture

One of the most intriguing characters involved with the Jacobite cause was Simon Lovat, the chief of the Clan Fraser. By the time of the '45 he was seventy-eight years old and had a reputation that few would envy. As a young man he had been involved in kidnapping and probably rape, and had worked for the Government before switching sides. He was looked on with suspicion by many of his compatriots. However, he had great influence in his own clan, having taken over as chief many years earlier through a process that was, to say the least, dubious. He had led them in the 1715 Rising, and in the '45 they were led once more in the Jacobite cause by his son. One incident in 1715 illustrated both his quick thinking and his essential bravery.

He was travelling through England while under a ban when one of his men let slip who he was. Word was passed to the local magistrate in Northallerton, who, hearing that the noted rebel Lord Lovat was on his patch, called out militia and surrounded the inn where Lovat and his party were. The magistrate burst into the inn, accompanied by several armed militia, to see Lovat sitting drinking with his friends at a table near the fire in the main room.

'Good heavens,' cried Lovat, getting to his feet, 'How are you? Don't say you can't remember me. I am Simon Campbell, the brother of the Duke of Argyll, we met at that horse race just the other year. Come in and have a drink with us.' How Simon knew that the duke and his brother had been at a nearby race-meeting the previous year is unclear but the poor magistrate was totally taken in by this charming Highland gentleman, and the rest of the night was spent in drinking toasts to the Hanoverian cause till at last the poor man was carried out and taken home, blind drunk! Simon and his friends carried on till the morning light then calmly made their way homewards.

The Jacobites on the Continent were extremely suspicious of him and Lovat later spent many years imprisoned in a French chateau for being a British spy, but that did nothing to curb his adventurous spirit. He might have been a slippery rogue, but he was known as a remarkably charming, intelligent and brave man. In the '45 his advanced age meant he could take little active part in the campaign, and it has been said that his advice, despite the political experience of a long life spent in plotting and counter-plotting, did not tend to be helpful to Prince Charlie's cause. He did, however, travel with the Jacobite army.

He managed to get away from the horrors of the battlefield at Culloden, travelling initially by coach and accompanied by about twenty of the Fraser clansmen. Having found that the house at Gortuleg to which he was fleeing had been taken by Redcoats he realised he would have to go into hiding. He got as far as the island on Loch Morar which had been the site of an illegal Catholic seminary at the time of the '15. Among his companions was the Catholic bishop, Hugh MacDonald. When they got to Loch Morar, Lovat had his kinsmen gather together every boat they could find on the loch. He then saw that they were towed them out to the island with them. Once this was done, they felt safe. Simon and his men stayed here throughout May, but then the situation changed.

It wasn't just soldiers who were scouring the Highlands for rebels; various naval ships were sailing up and down the West

Coast looking to intercept fleeing Jacobites and hopefully capture the greatest prize of all, Prince Charlie himself. The sloop *Furnace* was standing just off Morar, and when intelligence was received about Lovat's whereabouts a lifeboat from the sloop was dragged over the narrow strip of land between the loch and the sea. Just as the boat was reaching the loch a contingent of troops appeared at the west end of the loch.

Seeing the arrival of these Redcoats a local woman turned and said to her man, 'Ochone, ochone, there's the enemy at the river head and you know there are others on the island than the crooked one himself.' She clearly knew the reputation of the chief of the Clan Fraser.

'Dinnae fash,' replied her man, 'for every boat and plank on the loch is on that same island, and the holy one and the rest can laugh at the black ones and their guns.'

Out on the island, the Frasers saw the troops coming along the shoreline. They had plenty of food, there was a spring on the island and, having gathered up all the boats, they too were sure that their position was impregnable. So sure, in fact, that some of them began firing at the troops and shouting out insults. It was at that point that the lifeboat from the *Furnace* came into view on the loch and the situation was totally changed! Lord Lovat and the bishop at once got in one of the boats and were rowed to the southern shore of the loch, with the rest of their party coming in another boat behind them. They all disappeared into birch woods. The troops in the lifeboat landed on the island and proceeded to wreck everything inside the building, including holy books and sacred objects. They then set fire to the building itself.

Given the density of the woods on the south shore of the loch, the troops were reluctant to try and search for their prey amongst the birch trees. After all, they did not know the ground and the Frasers were well used to this sort of country. If they went after them they would almost certainly be ambushed. So, they simply spread out in groups around all the clachans and villages in the area and continued to search, sure that their quarry would turn up sooner or later. The Fraser contingent had split up, and Lovat himself decided to head for Meoble, six or seven miles up the loch. He was an old man and the journey took a lot out of him. It was more than a week later that he was discovered by a group of Redcoats, hiding in a cave with a strongbox full of gold. Somehow, the wily old devil had also managed to get his hands on two feather beds, so that even in the wild he could have some comfort. When taken he put up no fight. There was little an old man could do against heavily armed soldiers, and between five and six hundred guineas was found in his strongbox. Along with the troop who found him were some Highlanders, a couple of whom were pipers, and they played Lord Lovat's March as he was conveyed to the ship, though whether this was done to honour or mock him is unclear.

He was taken on the lifeboat down the loch and then, after crossing the narrow strip of land, was rowed out to the *Furnace*. The ship then raised anchor and sailed round the coast to land him at Loch Moidart. From there, he was put on a horse litter and taken with a considerable escort to Fort Augustus. He was, by now, in a poor condition because of both his age and having been forced to sleep outside, subsisting for some of the time on little more than sowens, or oats and water mixed together. There was no way he was fit to ride, so, once he had recovered sufficiently, he was sent off London by coach.

He had to wait a while before going on trial, but at last the date was set. His trial started on 9 March 1747. The long delay was a deliberate ploy to allow the prosecution enough time to gather sufficient evidence to ensure he was found guilty. There was no doubt of his guilt, and he had been heard to boast that there wasn't any plot to restore the Stewarts over the previous sixty years he hadn't had a hand in, though on whose behalf he never did say! Not for nothing was he known as *An Sionnach*, the fox: he had, in fact, left little evidence of any of his plotting. The wily old devil might have still got off with the charge of treason had it not been for John Murray of Broughton. He had been Prince Charlie's personal secretary throughout the campaign, and the threat of execution was enough to make him turn King's Evidence and betray his former companions. He had even informed the Government of how to get their hands on some of the letters Lovat had written to the prince. This established his role in the rebellion beyond all doubt, and he was found guilty. However, given his age, and his rank, he wasn't sentenced to be hung, drawn and quartered like so many of his fellow Jacobites. He was to be given the much lighter sentence of being beheaded! Such was the mercy of the Hanoverian court.

Once the verdict had been announced, Lovat drew himself to his feet and addressed the judges, saying, 'Farewell, my lords, we shall not all meet again in the same place. I am sure of that.' However, he had no intention of meekly accepting his fate. He penned a letter to the Duke of Cumberland himself reminding him that Lovat had often played with him when he was a child in the parks at Kensington and Hampton Court and had been of considerable service to the British Government, and to the House of Hanover, in years gone by. He received no reply and once he was sure of his fate he accepted the situation with remarkable courage, constantly making jokes about his forthcoming end.

On the way to his execution on Tower Hill on 9th April 1747, the route was thronged with cheering crowds. One woman, past the first flush of her youth, ran out of the crowd and jumped on the running board of the coach he was being transported in.

Sticking her head through the window she shouted, 'You'll get that nasty head of yours chopped off, you ugly old Scotch dog.'

Back came the answer, without even a second's hesitation, 'I believe I shall, you ugly old English bitch.'

When he was taken out to the scaffold he looked round at the seething crowd and asked with a raised eyebrow, 'God save us! Why should there be such a bustle about taking off an old grey head from a man who cannot get up three steps without two assistants?' Just at that, a stand full of spectators collapsed, creating a temporary halt to the proceedings. On being informed that several people had been killed and even more injured, he said with a wry smile, 'The more mischief, the better sport.'

He played his part right to the end, testing the edge of the executioner's axe for sharpness before saying to him, 'Now be sure and make a good job of it. I shall be most displeased if you don't!' All of this brought appreciative cheers from the watching crowds, and just before he died he called to his friends there present to be cheerful. 'After all,' he said, 'I am cheerful myself.'

His last words as he lay with his head on the block were 'Dulce et decorum est pro patria mori', which translates as 'It is sweet and right to die for one's country.' Considering his chequered past and life-long double-dealing, it was a real piece of bravura from the Old Fox, and totally in character.

The ultimate sacrifice

⟫◦⟪

Major James Lockhart of Cholmondley's Regiment was captured by the Jacobites at the Battle of Falkirk. He soon managed to escape, by bribing a guard, and headed back to England. He was in action at Culloden in April, and about a month and a half later he arrived in Glenmoriston, on the south-west shore of Loch Ness, with a company of Redcoats. As the soldiers came into the glen itself they passed a field where three men were busy harrowing. They were John MacDonald and Hugh Fraser, men in their sixties, and Hugh's son James, who had never set foot more than a mile or two outside the glen. They were simply going about their business and bothering no one when Lockhart ordered his men to shoot them. No word of warning, no threatening behaviour towards the Redcoats, no suggestion that any of them had even been rebels, just the simple command to kill them. Leaving the bodies lying where they fell, the Government troops headed further into the glen.

The troops then came to the farm of Grant of Dundreggan, and Lockhart had him dragged out of his house before his family.

'Right,' he barked at Grant, 'you will now gather up all the cattle in this area and bring them here to me.'

Grant was sent off with a group of soldiers accompanying him, and the rest of the troops went on a rampage of looting and destruction along the glen, burning houses and destroying crops, all without any suggestion that the people being thus persecuted had any Jacobite sympathies. Lockhart picked the most comfortable house in the glen for his own headquarters, simply turning out the women and children who lived there on to the hillside. His men similarly took over those houses that took their fancy, throwing the occupants out to fend for themselves as they might. All that night the glen was filled with the cries of bewildered children, the shrieks of women who had been assaulted and worse, and the shouts of soldiers moving through the flickering shadows cast by the burning houses. Many of the soldiers were drunk, making free with the whisky and beer they found as they went about their evil work. For many of the Glenmoriston people it was as if all at once they had been thrust into hell itself, while still alive.

The following morning Lockhart went back to Dundreggan, and, hearing that Grant had not managed to gather in all of the glen's cattle, he showed his character. He had Grant stripped naked, tied hand and foot, and then, as he lay on the ground near his own front door, he had his men bring the bodies of the three men shot the previous day and hang them by their feet from a nearby tree. It was only the intercession of one Captain Grant of Loudon's Regiment that stopped Lockhart killing Grant there and then, and he satisfied himself with burning the house at Dundreggan. He then stripped Grant's wife of her rings and her clothes!

Around the same time, one of the Frasers was making his way back from visiting the Presbyterian minister at Kilmorack, further up the glen. Seeing the way things had been going, he had asked the minister to write him a paper stating that he had not been a rebel, that he was a Presbyterian and that he was loyal to the house of Hanover. He was coming through a stream towards the soldiers, waving the paper from the minister, when he was shot dead by them.

So they advanced westwards along the glen, burning and

pillaging as they went. Women were stripped of their clothing and raped, both young and old, and even a couple who were quite obviously pregnant. Houses were burned indiscriminately and every piece of livestock rounded up and sent to Fort Augustus. Men, women and children fled into the hills, and, as the destruction went on, some of them died from exposure. It was as the troops neared *Ceann-na Croc*, a great rock at the foot of the northern slopes of *Beinn na Eoin*, overlooking the River Moriston, that they spotted Roderick MacKenzie. Like many of his kin, he had been out in the '45, but he stood apart from all the other Jacobites because of one particular fact. He was the same age, height and build, and had the same colouring and shape of face as Prince Charles Edward Stewart. It was something that was remarked on constantly through the heady times of 1745 and 1746. After the disbanding of the Jacobite army at Ruthven Barracks, he headed back to his own country around Glenmoriston, where, like many others he was forced to hide out in the hills. Sometimes he would hide in one of the caves in the locality, sometimes he would creep into barns or outhouses, and sometimes he would build a simple shelter in the woods. At times he had been forced to sleep on the side of a hill in the cold air of the mountain nights. This was not as bad as it sounds, for the plaid that most Highlanders wore provided a warm blanket once it was taken off and wrapped around the body. Now, the rebels like Roderick were in their own clan lands and had relations living in the clachans and small villages that were being methodically searched and pillaged by the Redcoats. They also had their own information network.

So it was that Roderick had heard, just a day or so earlier, that the prince himself was somewhere around Glenmoriston, heading for the west coast where he hoped to get on board a ship that would take him to France.

He was greatly distressed to hear this, as the area was covered with roaming groups of British soldiers, and when later that same day he saw Lockhart with some of his Redcoats in the glen below him, he had no hesitation. He leapt from his hiding place in a small copse of trees and began to head, none too quickly, on a course parallel to the soldiers. It was only a matter of a minute or so before he was seen and heard the shout, 'Hold fast, who goes there?' At once, he began to run off up the glen.

The soldiers immediately gave chase. He ran as far as the great rock of *Ceann-na-Croc*, where he turned to face them, sword in hand. He was an able swordsman, but, outnumbered as he was, about twelve to one, he could not hope to last long. He had no intention of surrendering. After receiving half a dozen minor blows, but sorely wounding a couple of the Redcoats, he at last took a blow straight through his chest. He knew it was fatal one, and as he slumped to the ground he had just enough breath to gasp, 'Alas, alas, you have killed your prince.' He then fell dead at the feet of the soldiers, who all stood back at these words.

Some of them were worried that they had committed regicide, for the idea that there was something almost superhuman about royalty still held sway in many minds, but Lockhart spoke up.

'Never fear, men,' he said, 'this has been a good days' work. This man was a pretender to the throne and a traitor to the true king. We have faithfully fulfilled the orders of the legal king and I am sure we will be well rewarded.'

He then gave orders for the head of the corpse to be cut off and the body buried close to the great rock of *Ceann-na-Croc*. Now, as in those days taking heads was a common means of identifying the deceased, none of the soldiers thought much about it. Word of the death of the prince went like wildfire round the Government troops in and around Glenmoriston and all search parties were recalled. They had got their prey and the commanders were sure that this would put a stop to all rebel activity. The stragglers in the hills who didn't surrender once they heard their leader was dead could be picked off at their leisure. They reckoned that the campaign was effectively over. The local people knew different, for a few of them were allowed to see the head of the supposed prince to let them understand that any further resistance to the Redcoats was futile. Of course, it had the opposite effect. All were made proud, but saddened, by the brave death of Roderick Mackenzie, but they knew fine well that it gave the fugitive prince an increased chance of escaping to France and, maybe, just maybe, returning at a later date to raise the clans again. The head was taken to the local commander in Fort Augustus and it was shown to MacDonald of Kingsburgh, who confirmed that it was the prince. However, this did not convince the Duke of Cumberland, who took the head with him when he went to London.

Richard Morison, valet to the prince, was in Carlisle prison under sentence of death and Cumberland sent for him to be brought to London. Like many of the Jacobite prisoners, he had been badly treated, badly fed and had fallen ill. By the time he could be brought to London the head had rotted beyond recognition, and there was little point in even showing it to the poor man. Word had got out, however, that the prince was still alive and that the head had been that of a loyal follower who had sacrificed himself for Prince Charlie. This, combined with the ongoing failure of the thirty-thousand-pound reward to tempt anyone into betraying the prince, served only to increase the brutality with which the Redcoats treated the Highlanders.

It was quite a few weeks before word came to the troops in Glenmoriston that they had been fooled, and it was too late: the prince had made the coast and embarked on the *Heureux* for France. Roderick's ultimate sacrifice also saved Richard Morison's life as well for, taken under sentence of death from Carlisle, he was given a pardon when he reached London and allowed to make his ways safely to France.

Today, Mackenzie's Cairn marks the scene of Roderick's brave last stand, about half a mile east of the confluence of the Moriston and Doe rivers.

Father Munro

In eighteenth-century Scotland, as in the rest of the United Kingdom, there were laws forbidding Catholics from celebrating Mass. Other laws made it an offence to disseminate Catholic literature and to harbour a priest or even to arrange any gathering of Catholics for religious purposes. Scottish Catholics lived in a constant state of fear as their houses could be raided at any time to see if they were keeping any of the accoutrements of their faith, like altar-cloths, icons and the like. It was even forbidden for Catholics to inherit or bequeath property. Some of the laws were quite petty and spiteful, such as the one that made it illegal for any Catholic to own more than one horse! In some parts of the country a certain amount of tolerance was shown, but in others the full force of the law was repeatedly brought to bear against Catholics.

MacLean of Coll, an elder of the Presbyterian Kirk, was criticised for not pursuing 'Papists' with enough zeal. Coll, like many of the islands and much of the Highlands, had a great many Catholics, and, the Sunday following this criticism, Maclean actually stood at a crossroads where the roads that ran to the chapel and the kirk met and physically knocked down all who dared take the chapel road. In many parts of the country attempts were made to get Catholics to renounce their faith and send their children to Presbyterian schools. It is a remarkable testament to their faith that so many successfully resisted such persecution.

However badly the Catholic laity were treated, for priests it was even worse.

They could be arrested, any place, at any time, and then banished. If they returned, they could be sentenced to death. There was a reward of five hundred merks, a substantial sum equivalent to around three hundred and fifty pounds, for anyone who told the authorities about the presence of a priest. Many of them were effectively permanently on the run, ministering to their flocks while under the constant threat of being arrested and imprisoned. It was considered unsafe for any priest in Scotland to sleep two nights in the same bed. Despite this, there were many remarkably brave men who continued to tend to their congregations, mainly in the Highlands. Some of them were caught and banished on more than one occasion, and their tenacity in returning into danger is commendable, no matter what one may think of their beliefs.

There was even a Catholic seminary in Loch Morar, although it only lasted for a year after it was opened in 1714. However, it was replaced by one at Scalan in 1732, where it survived for another 89 years, its presence kept a secret from Government agents and Protestant ministers by the Catholic Highlanders living around it. In matters of religion, the divergence between most of the Highlands and the Lowlands of Scotland was, of course, considerable.

Robert Munro was a Catholic priest and showed considerable courage and remarkable stubbornness. Born in Ross-shire, he became a priest in 1671. In 1688 he was in Knoydart, and shortly after William of Orange came to the throne he was arrested and put on trial in Edinburgh. His crime was simply that of being a priest and administering Catholic rites to those who wanted them. The prosecution of Catholics was a rigorous affair in those days and he was found guilty – he could hardly deny his cloth – and was banished from Britain. Soon, he turned up in the Protestant

Low Countries, where he ended up in prison in Ghent after being arrested for conspiring against William, Prince of Orange, who was about to become King of England. Luckily, Munro had some influential friends among the tiny Catholic community there, and they managed to secure his release after a few years, most probably through the time-honoured process of money changing hands. From Ghent, Munro boarded a ship heading for London, with the intention of trying to make his way back to Scotland to fulfil what he clearly saw as his duty to the Catholic people of Knoydart. As soon as he landed he was arrested, all of his money was confiscated and he was thrown into a jail: not a pleasant experience even today but ten times worse back in the seventeenth century.

After a year he was brought out of the stinking hole where he had been kept in Newgate prison, and once more he was put on trial, found guilty and banished. However, he was nothing if not a determined character, and once on the Continent he headed to Dunkirk, where he managed to locate a ship that was sailing directly to Scotland. Landing on the east coast, he travelled across the country in disguise, and at last he managed to get back to his parishioners, who were overjoyed to have their own priest back with them. The situation hadn't changed: he was still effectively an outlaw, and he had to keep an eye out for Government troops, who at this time were regularly patrolling the Highlands with the intention of suppressing any thoughts of further rebellion amongst the natives. There was also the problem of potential informants, for not everyone in Knoydart was a Catholic, and the possibility was always there that one of his own flock would be tempted by the rewards that were available for those prepared to tell the authorities of the presence of a priest.

With the help and support of his parishioners, he managed to carry on his priestly duties. Such was the danger, though, that he was constantly on the move and, when not administering the sacrament, giving the last rites and performing marriages etc., usually in people's houses, he was constantly in disguise. Often enough, he had to hide out in a wee cave, little more than a fox's den, between Dorlin and Port a Bhata. It was no more than eight to nine feet long, roughly five feet at its highest and cold and damp, but such was Father Robert's commitment that he was never heard to complain. Keeping his ministry in these conditions, when, despite the best efforts of his loyal flock, he was often hungry and cold, shows just how deep his commitment to his faith must have been.

Occasionally, he would meet up with other priests, particularly Father Ryan and Father Devoir, who lived the same outlaw life in the West. In 1696, Ryan was captured and his treatment showed that the Government was becoming less and less tolerant of the priest in the hills. Ryan was not banished from the country but thrown into prison and effectively left to die. Two years later, Father Devoir was also captured by Government troops and suffered exactly the same fate. By now, Father Robert knew that if caught again he too would be thrown into prison with no hope of rescue. However, he carried on as before. He continued to minister to the Catholic population of Knoydart and, with the death of his fellow priests, was called on to service a much wider area. The constant travelling, hiding out and perhaps the tension of permanently being on the look-out began to take its toll, and in 1704 he was stricken with a fever that laid him up for a few weeks. He could not be moved and so it was that he was found by a group of British Government troops in a hut halfway up a hill in Glengarry. They were on the lookout for Catholic priests and Father Robert was once more arrested and this time imprisoned in a nearby castle. Here he was thrown into a dungeon and left with no medical assistance at all, and within a matter of days he died, alone in a prison cell, but sure in his heart that he had done his very best to serve both his God and his parishioners in Knoydart.

Better it burn

⫸◆⫷

Allan Dearg was the chief of the Clanranald MacDonalds at the turn of the eighteenth century. He had fought alongside Viscount Claverhouse at Killiecrankie and never renounced his loyalty to the Stewart cause. In the years after 1689, the Government did its best to prevent further trouble arising in the Highlands. Some of its actions, like the shocking massacre of Glencoe, were meant to discourage the Highland warrior clans from taking up their weapons against the House of Hanover, but there were also other ways of trying to tame the clans. One of these was to use bribery. The general policy was to buy off those who could be bought, while at the same time letting it be understood that, if it were felt necessary, the last resort would be to exterminate all those who would not submit. It was a policy that, in time, worked.

Not until General Wade drove his roads into the Highlands in the 1730s was there any real possibility of a final successful military action against the clans loyal to the House of Stewart, and bribery was of little use amongst the clans loyal to the Jacobite cause. The rugged mountains and twisting glens were much more suited to the Highland warrior's skills, honed through centuries of cattle-raiding and feuding, than the regimented fighting style of the British Army, even if it was the most efficient fighting force on the planet at the time. So the Government's hopes of subjugating the Highlands in the early years of the eighteenth century failed and the Jacobite cause continued to flourish, just as it was kept going in many Lowland areas. And one of those keeping the fire of the Jacobite cause burning in the mountains was Allan Dearg.

His anti-Government feelings were only increased by the occupation of his ancestral home, Castle Tioram on the Moidart peninsula, by a garrison of troops for many years after the troubles of the late 1680s. There seemed no immediate hope of further action against the Hanoverians, so, like many another man raised in the warrior tradition of the Highland clans, Allan Dearg left his homeland and enlisted in the French Army. At the time, there were half-a-dozen regiments in the French Army formed from exiled Scots and Irish, and they found ready recruits amongst Highland regiments sent to serve in the Low Countires. In the War of Spanish Succession, Allan Dearg fought against the British under the leadership of the Duke of Berwick and was prominent in the Battle of Almanza in April 1707, which gave the Franco-Spanish forces almost total control of the Iberian peninsula. He was well to the fore in the battle, using all the sword-fighting skills of the Highland warrior, but in the course of the action he was wounded several times.

As he lay on the battlefield, unable to move because of the severity of his wounds, he was found by a search party and carried off to a nearby country house, where it was at first thought that he would not survive. However, he came through the crisis, and it was at this period that he made the acquaintance of Penelope Mackenzie, daughter of Colonel Mackenzie, who had served as the Governor of Tangiers for the French Government. After he had recuperated, the pair married, and they came back to live on the island of Uist. This was a dangerous thing to do, as there is little doubt that British Government spies would have known that Allan Dearg had been serving in the French Army. Amongst his own people in the far off island of Uist, however, he felt safe and lived quietly till matters once more came to a head in the Rising of

1715. It was not long before this that the Government troops at last left Castle Tioram.

Now, there was a great deal of plotting going among the Jacobites in the first two decades of the eighteenth century, and Allan was privy to much of it. He had already shown his loyalty to the cause, and his experience as a soldier made him a man of considerable importance. However, he well knew that there was a problem. In the year of 1715, one man was becoming more and more important to the Jacobite cause in Scotland than any other. This was Bobbing John Erskine, Earl of Mar, a man whose military experience was nil. He was also a man whose character left much to be desired. His nickname is thought to have referred to his indecision and his habit of changing his mind. He had been an active member of the British Government and was one of those appointed to oversee the implementation of the Act of Union in 1707, an Act that was despised by many in Scotland, and not just Jacobites. In 1708, when James Stewart made his abortive attempt to land in Scotland, Mar was active on behalf of the British Government, even going as far as to hand over to the authorities a list of known Jacobites in the north-east of Scotland, where the Episcopalian religion was strong. Episcopalians, like Catholics, were usually staunch Jacobites, seeing in the Stewarts the best chance for their own brand of the Christian religion to flourish. In 1711, Mar had become Secretary of State for Scotland, effectively the Crown's representative in Scotland. In 1714, Queen Anne, who was the daughter of James II, and as a Protestant, the last Stewart to occupy the British throne, died. Mar then wrote to the new king, George, at his home in Hanover, to remind him of the service that he had given to the crown. His approaches were spurned by the new king. It was this rejection that seems to have finally convinced Bobbing John to espouse the Jacobite cause. He was, of course, a major political figure and, as such, of great importance to the exiled king, but those who, like Allan Dearg, realised there was a lot of fighting to do trusted neither his abilities as a leader or even his loyalty to the Stewart cause.

Yet if James Stewart chose the Earl of Mar to lead the Jacobite forces in Scotland Allan Dearg would support him as best he could. He had no hesitation in raising the Clanranald MacDonalds on behalf of the Old Pretender, or James VII, as the Jacobites thought of him. He returned to Castle Tioram to take command of a force of over five hundred MacDonald clansmen. Before setting off with his men to join up with the rest of the MacDonalds under Glengarry and become part of the Jacobite army, he had one task he felt he had to perform. He called one of his closest cousins and most trusted friends to him.

'Lachlan,' he said in sad voice, 'I have a heavy duty to ask of you this day. When we march off to join the cause I want you to stay here and set fire to Castle Tioram.'

'For heaven's sake, man, why?' gasped the astonished Lachlan.

'Well, you know that the foul red-coated swine have been camping out here for many years. Once the country is up again, I have little doubt that they will most likely want to re-garrison the castle. They can keep it supplied from the sea and it won't take them long to try and land men here. So, I want you to make sure that when they get here there is nothing that will be of any help to them,' Allan replied.

'But what of yourself when you return? There is every chance the cause will triumph, and you could come back and live in the home of your ancestors,' Lachlan pleaded.

'No, I will not be returning. I have just enough of the second sight to know my time has come. I will see Castle Tioram and the hills and islands no more once I leave. I am sure of it. So, Lachlan, please do as I ask. Better it burn than serve the needs of our enemies,' and, as he said this, he looked deep into his cousin's eyes. Lachlan realised just how serious the chief was. He nodded. It would be done.

So it was that a short while later, as the great contingent of the MacDonald clan made their way east through the gorge of Scardoish, Allan Dearg MacDondald stopped and sat for a while. The spot was long known as *Aite-suidhe vich ish Aileien*, or the spot where the chief of Clanranald sat and looked for the last time over the shining waters of Loch Moidart and the beautiful islands of the Hebrides. When he reached Perth and went to see Mar he told him, 'My family have been, on such occasions as we now find ourselves coming to, ever wont to be the first on the field of battle, and the last to leave it.' Mar knew well the reputation of the MacDonalds in battle, and in Allan Dearg knew he had a thoroughly able and well-trained soldier and leader of men. But Allan's foreboding had been right and he never did make it back to Moidart or the Hebrides

At the fateful battle of Sheriffmuir, Clanranald was just about to lead his men in the fearsome Highland charge when a musket ball took him in the chest. He was carried, dying, from the field, and for a moment the men of Clanranald faltered. It had long been a tradition that when a Highland chief fell in battle his men would take him home to be buried, and many of them wanted to show this respect for their kinsman and leader. At that moment, however, Glengarry, leader of the rest of the MacDonalds, realised what was happening and ran in front of them, waving his bonnet and crying at the top of his voice, 'Revenge! Revenge today and sorrow to-morrow!' This rallied the Clanranald men, and they fell on the opposing Government troops with such fury that they routed them. It was this success on the left wing of the Jacobite army, as opposed to the chaos on the other wing, that gave some veneer of respectability to the actions of the Jacobite army that day, and prevented a government victory over considerably superior forces.

With the death of their chief, the Clanranald warriors had little further wish for battle, but it was not their actions, but those of the Earl of Mar, already planning to flee the country, that saw the rebellion fizzle out. Clanranald fell before he could see this pathetic display. However, he did leave behind him a reputation as a great warrior, and a gallant and generous man, and when the word of his death reached the West Coast and the Isles there was great sorrow amongst all who had known, or even just heard, of him, such was his reputation as a right and proper chief.

Appearances can be deceptive

⟫◆⟪

In July 1746, the red-coated army of the British Government was sweeping through the Highlands trying to root out rebels. There was widespread brutality, rape and murder, much of it carried out by Scots loyal to the Government, or, in some cases, simply looking to have revenge on traditional enemies. Stewart Shaw of Inch-Croy, just north of Culloden Moor, had been out with the Mackintoshes in support of the prince and had gone into hiding after the battle. His wife and three daughters were left helpless at Inch-Croy. Times were hard, but they were lucky and had been spared the vicious excesses of the Hanoverian troops after the battle and in the weeks afterwards. Living so close to the battle-field where so much slaughter had been carried out, they reckoned they had been fortunate indeed. However, one day that July, a tall, powerful, red-headed Highlander came to their door claiming to be one Sergeant Campbell, sent to search the house for the rebel Shaw. He was fully armed with sword and pistols and had a targe slung across his back.

Mrs Shaw, like so many Scots women down the centuries, was a woman of spirit and said, 'I would far rather a dozen of the Government's Hessian mercenaries tramped through my house than one such as you, a Campbell and a traitor to his own king and people.'

'Och well, Mrs Shaw,' the man replied with a crooked smile, 'that's as may be, but I am thinking you will fare better at the

145

hands of one of your own countrymen than at the hands of the Germans, or even the English soldiers. Now, will you be giving me the keys to the house or not?'

Mrs Shaw was well aware there was little she and her daughters could do against this big Campbell, armed as he was. So she disdainfully flung the keys to the house at his feet. Picking them up he began to methodically search the house, stopping regularly to look out of various windows, and all the time Mrs Shaw kept up a barrage of insults, to which he paid not the slightest attention. At last, he came to main bedroom and was looking behind a large wardrobe he had pulled away from the wall when there was the sound of horses outside. At once, he turned and looked at the lady of the house, pointed silently at the head of her bed with his left hand and put the first finger of his right hand to his lips. She gazed at him in amazement as the sound of heavy boot-clad feet thundered up the stairs.

The door swung open and in came a red-coated officer with five dragoons behind him, all with sword or a pistol in hand.

'Right, now, what's going on here?' demanded the officer, his eyes swinging between Mrs Shaw and the big Highlander.

'I am so glad you are here, Sir,' blustered Mrs Shaw. 'This coarse ruffian of a sergeant has been turning everything topsy-turvy in searching the house. There is no one here but my daughters and I, and he refuses to accept it.'

The officer glared at the kilted man. 'Is that so. Right, you brute, be off with you. If there are any rebels here, I'll be answerable for them. Get out,' he spat at the kilted figure before him.

'Och no, I don't think so,' replied the Highlander, his right hand on the pistol in his belt. I have been commissioned to search the place and I was here before you. I have been issued with orders from headquarters and any reward coming is to be mine. As I have precedence you and your men can go.'

'What, you Scotch mongrel?' shouted the officer, going red in the face at this effrontery. 'Show me your commission then, this instant.'

'Och, I think you should be showing me your commission first if you are demanding mine,' replied the other in a calm and steady voice.

'I am Cornet Letham of Cobham's dragoons and have no need to show the likes of you anything. Now, who exactly is your commanding officer?' came the riposte.

'Well,' said the Highlander with a grim smile, 'I think I can say that I am under the orders of a better gentleman than yourself, or any that have ever commanded you,' smiled the Highlander.

'What?' shouted Letham. 'What did you say? One better than anyone who has ever commanded me? How dare you! That is treason and you, Sir, are clearly a damned rebel. I arrest you as such here and now.'

So saying, he came forward and, sure in the knowledge that he had five armed men at his back, he grabbed the tall man by the throat. He did not know his opponent, who whipped out his pistol, swung back his right arm and gave the officer a thunderbolt of a blow to the side of his head with the weapon. As the officer fell lifeless to the floor, his men levelled their pistols at the red-headed man, but with remarkable speed he leapt behind the wardrobe drawing his other pistol as he did so. Now without a clear shot at him the dragoons were in a bit of a fix. The doorway to the room was narrow and only one man at a time could come through it. That man would be an easy target for the Highlander, protected as he was by the solid wood of the press. It was a stand–off.

After a whispered conversation, two of the dragoons went outside. Their plan was to get at their enemy through the small window in the room. As soon as they were at the window and had smashed the glass they were sure they had him. They couldn't see him behind the press, but if he moved they would shoot him down and their friends could now safely come into the room. They didn't know their enemy though.

Realising what was happening, he replaced his pistols in his belt and with his left hand took out his dirk, that vicious and most useful weapon and tool of the Highland warrior. Then, he simply took his blue bonnet, put it over the handle of his dirk and just showed the edge of it round the corner of the heavy press. At once, both dragoons at the window, keen to get in a fatal shot, let fire. Just as the bullets tore through his bonnet the Highlander leapt out from his position and out through the doorway swinging with his sword in one hand and his dirk in the other. He came at the soldiers at the door so fast they had no time to fire their pistols, and the sight of the whirling steel terrified them and they took to their heels. They were veterans and realised that in the enclosed space the sweeping blades of the big Highlander were fatal. They ran for the door, tugging at their swords. Once outside, they thought they would soon cut him down. But they never had a chance. In their heavy coats and great boots they were no match for the man bearing down on them, and two of them were chopped down before they even reached the door to the outside. The third man looked over his shoulder to see his companions fall and ran off down the road. He hadn't gone more than few yards before he, too, was cut down. The other two, who had been at the window, came round the corner of the house in time to see their comrade fall and made for their horses.

The red-headed Highlander saw this and, as they mounted and took off, he leapt on the officer's horse and chased after them, shouting on them to turn and fight. The chase was seen by a couple of local lads, Peter Grant and Alexander McEachan, who were hiding-out in the heather above the house. Often in later years they told of the Highlander flailing at his horse with the flat of his sword trying to catch up with the two red-coats. He might have been a great fighter but as a horseman he was no match for professional horsemanship of the dragoons, and in his efforts to catch up with them he eventually rode into a boggy bit of ground and was thrown by the horse. Picking himself up, he looked after the fleeing soldiers then turned to run back to Inch-Croy. By the time he was nearing the house the two observers had run down from the hill and were waiting for him by the door of the house.

'Well done,' said McEachan with a smile and holding out his hand, 'that was a grand chase. Pity you didn't catch up with them, though, Colonel.'

'Aye, right enough,' came the reply as the red-headed man shook McEachan by the hand. He had recognised the two of them from a fair way off as men who had loyally followed his command throughout the abortive campaign to England and back. At this point, Mrs Shaw and her daughters came out from the out-building they had run to for shelter when the trouble had started.

'So you are no Campbell after all, then,' she said sternly.

'Colonel John Roy Stewart at your service,' he said, doffing his bullet-torn bonnet from off his head in a sweeping bow.

Mrs Shaw was much relieved, for her heart had almost stopped when he had pointed at the head of the bed just as the troops had arrived. They now went in and moved the bed to reveal a concealed door behind which was a hidden room. In the room, which was extremely cramped and windowless, along with Shaw himself were Captain Finlayson and MacDonald of Lochgarry. They had heard all the noise but thought it better to stay where they were as they had no way of seeing what was happening. All were glad to shake hands with their rescuer.

'But why, for heaven's sake, did you tell me you were a Campbell,' asked Mrs Shaw.

'Well,' replied Stewart, 'I had seen the dragoons coming and

149

was just intent on getting here before them, but, when they did come, as long as you thought I was one of those damned Hanoverians I had a chance of getting the better of them. I didn't fancy taking on six men without some kind of delay. If you hadn't said I was one of them it was likely they would have shot me down as soon as they came into the house. I am sorry for having to deceive you though ma'am.'

'I am more than glad that you did, Sir,' she said, 'for you have certainly done well by us all this day. But you had better all be off quick for those dragoons will be back with a great many of their accomplices before too long.'

And so it was that the six Jacobites headed off from Inch-Croy, Shaw himself unsure of when, or even if, he would see his home, his beloved wife and his lovely daughters again. He, Finlayson, MacEachan and Grant successfully made their way with the help of friends, through the Highlands to Glasgow, where they managed to get aboard foreign ships and escape. Colonel Stewart and Lochgarry went west to join the prince, and then they too left their beloved Scotland for France.

As for Mrs Shaw and her daughters, well, they had a hard time of it when Cumberland heard that a single Highlander had bested six of his troops, killing four of them in the process. He made sure that Inch-Croy was looted and burned, all the stock slaughtered and the family of Shaw locked up in prison for many months. But they never did manage to catch Colonel Stewart!

A Highland cross dresser

Donald MacLaren of Wester Invernentie in Balquhidder was a captain in the Appin Regiment of the Jacobite army in the '45. The regiment was composed mainly of Stewarts and MacLarens, with a sprinkling of McColls and other small septs. Under the leadership of Charles Stewart of Ardshiel, the Appin Regiment had a significant role in the defeat of General Cope at Prestonpans in September 1745. They went on with the Jacobite army into England, following it through the long retreat to Scotland and defeat at Culloden. During this overwhelming defeat for the Jacobite cause, seventeen men sacrificed themselves in protecting the standard of the Stewart clan before one of the regiment, Donald Livingston, cut the flag from its staff and carried it away.

Although Donald was wounded in the battle he managed to get away from the battlefield, unlike so many of his countrymen, who were executed in cold blood where they lay, on the direct orders of the Duke of Cumberland. Despite his wounds, Donald managed to make his way south through the mountains to his native Balquhidder, where he hid out in the hills to the north of Ben Ledi while slowly recovering from his injuries. In this period virtually every glen in Scotland, outside the Campbell heartland of Argyll, was garrisoned by Redcoat troops, as were many villages and towns throughout the whole country, including Aberdeen, Dundee and Stirling. The Government was taking no chances on the rebellion bursting out again, and almost of all of

Scotland was under direct military rule till well into the 1750s. As well as the garrisons in the glens, there were troops of mounted dragoons regularly patrolling the passes through the Highlands. The official line was that this was to stop cattle-raiding, a long-established Highland tradition, but in fact it was part of a policy of not only keeping a lid on the Highlands but destroying the ancient clan system, which kept thousands of armed men in a state of almost constant readiness for battle.

The long-term pacification of the Highlands, which Scottish monarchs had been trying to implement for centuries, was at last a viable project. It also meant that fugitive Jacobites, even with the support of the local population, had to be careful, very careful, not to be caught. One day, in the spring of 1746, Donald was just not careful enough. He was on the Braes of Leny, overlooking the road to Loch Lubnaig, when he was spotted by a patrol. As he was wearing Highland dress and carrying weapons – both of which were, of course, banned by the Disarming Act of 1746 – the troops immediately chased him. They caught up with him and, after a short fight in which he was badly wounded, he was disarmed and made prisoner. This time, his recuperation was to take place in the confines of a cell in the nearby market town of Crieff, rather than in the clear, fresh air of his beloved hills. He was, of course, thoroughly searched after being captured but, in one of the folds of his plaid, a *sgian dubh*, the small dark knife of the Highlander, was missed. The fact that the soldiers had already taken two of these little knives from him meant they missed this third one.

Donald was kept prisoner at Crieff till he was fit enough to travel, and then he was to be sent to Carlisle, where many of his fellow Jacobites had already been through the so-called judicial process of the time. It was a foregone conclusion that he would be found guilty of treason; the only question was whether he would be executed or transported to the West Indies to work as a slave in the blistering sun. Trying the rebels in England meant that there was no need to acknowledge the differences between English and Scots law, the latter of which, as we have seen, had no discretion to sentence anyone to transportation. Now, Donald was well aware of what was about to happen – all of Scotland knew what happened to Jacobites taken to Carlisle – and he had been thinking about how best to escape while he was regaining his strength in the cell in Crieff. Although by the time he was to be taken to Carlisle his wound had almost healed completely, he made a show of still being very weak, and was apparently falling asleep at all times of the day.

It was therefore decided that he should be taken off to Carlisle on horseback, tied to the dragoon sitting in front of him. The rest of the party was made up of a dozen prisoners, the same number of soldiers and another five dragoons. From almost the moment they left Crieff, Donald made a great show of constantly nodding his head and falling onto the shoulder of the dragoon as if asleep. It didn't take long for the dragoon to stop nudging him to keep him awake and let him lie slumped against his back. This carried on all through the first few days that he was being transported, and all the time Donald was keeping an eye open for an opportunity to make his move.

At last, several days into the journey and already a fair distance from the Highlands, he realised his chance was about to come. It was a cold and misty afternoon and the troop of soldiers and prisoners was heading down through the Southern Uplands towards Moffat, on a route close to today's A701. Donald had been this way before, on his return from Derby, and remembered the lie of the land. He and the dragoon were bringing up the rear of the straggling column. In those days the road ran along the top of the Devil's Beef Tub, a deep cauldron-like hollow in the hills through which runs a brisk stream that flows into the River Annan. Trying his best to stay relaxed till the last possible second, Donald pretended to be asleep, slumped against the dragoon's back, and waited till they were directly above the stream which rolled and tumbled down the precipitous slope of the Beef Tub. Then, in an instant, he slipped out his *sgian dubh*, cut through the rope tying him to the dragoon, leapt from the horse and rolled down the slope into the stream. He was gone in a flash, and the dragoon gave out a yell to alert his comrades as he pulled up his horse and turned to see little more than a flash of tartan as Donald rolled down the slope and into the mist. The troops halted and the prisoners were lined up with levelled muskets pointed at them while the dragoons dismounted to climb down after the escapee. By the time they were coming down the hillside, hampered a bit by their heavy boots, Donald had made his way to a boggy pool near the bottom of the hollow. Here, he stood up to his neck in the water close by the bank, and using his trusty *sgian dubh* he cut a large slice of turf, which he placed on his head. He could see little of the bank opposite, but from any more than a foot or two away he was invisible. For almost an hour he stood there in the chill water as the dragoons passed back and forward, slashing at the tussocks of grass with their swords and cursing more and more.

At last, at a command from their officer, the dragoons gave up and headed back up to convoy the rest of their prisoners on their miserable journey. Waiting a good while longer to ensure no one had stayed behind, Donald at last hauled himself out of the water. He was chilled to the bone, but wringing out his plaid he wrapped it about his body and climbed out of the Devil's Beef Tub and up the slopes of Clyde Law, heading north. The story of his daring escape soon spread around the area, and for a long time after the locals referred to the spot where he made his escape as MacLaurin's Leap.

His luck was in that day for within a couple of hours he came across the carcass of a sheep that had recently fallen from a crag above. He sliced up as much of the beast as he could carry and stashed it inside his plaid. He knew better than light a fire, but the raw lamb, sliced thinly to aid chewing, would keep him going till he managed to get closer to home. Carefully keeping to cover wherever possible, and making sure he would never show clearly against the skyline, Donald slowly moved north, regularly stopping to look around and using all the skills he had learned in the hills of his native Balquhidder to avoid being seen. Through the hills he went, past the great fire hill of Tinto near Biggar and on over the bleak moors to the west of the Pentland Hills. As he got closer to Stirling he travelled only by night, and at last he managed to pass Stirling, heading on up the Forth toward the Fords of Frew. Here, he crossed over the ancient ford and headed towards Callander, though by now his stock of food was gone. This did not bother him; he was close to home and knew where he could find friends he could trust. It was only a matter of another day or two before he was back on the Braes of Balquhidder, and he had no intention of leaving again. What with being out fighting in the Jacobite army and then being in prison, he had had enough of adventure. Now he only wanted to spend the rest of his life peacefully in the area he had been raised in.

There is an old cliché about the burnt child fearing the fire, and Donald MacLaren was all too aware that he would have to be careful from now on. In fact, the Highlands were garrisoned for nearly another decade. The idea of permanently hiding out in the hills held little appeal so Donald, clearly a man of some intelligence, decided on another approach. He was fair haired, slim and not too tall, and, as he had never had to shave more than once every few days, he decided he could turn his appearance to his advantage. So it was that the stock of bonny Highland lassies on the Braes of Balquhidder was increased by one. Well, not that bonny, for though Donald could pass for a woman, even from quite close up, there was little chance that he would be taken for a beauty. So, for the next year, taking care to keep out of the way of passing Redcoats whenever possible, Donald lived as a woman with some of his female cousins. Whenever he had to go anywhere other than the clachan they all lived in, or if there were Redcoats or strangers about, he would pull his shawl over his head and try to walk as much like his cousins as he could. Not once was he stopped and questioned. It was great relief for him, though, when the General Indemnity of 1747 was passed and he could get out of wearing a woman's skirt and back into man's attire.

Loyal officers of the law

⟫◆⟪

In 1752 the army garrison at Braemar was under the command of Captain Charles Desclouseaux of the King's Regiment. His garrison consisted of himself, a subaltern, two sergeants, two corporals and three dozen privates. Their job was to enforce the Disarming Act and to try to arrest those Jacobites who had taken to the hills and were living the life of caterans. Some of these armed bands, not all of whom were as honest as they might have been, made a special point of stealing from Presbyterian ministers. Though there were some in the Highlands who supported the Government, the great majority of the local population supported the caterans. In June some of the Braemar soldiers out on patrol came across a man called MacPherson, who was dressed in the *breacan* or plaid. This was, of course, illegal under the Disarming Act of 1746, which prohibited the carrying of weapons and the wearing of traditional Highland dress. A few days later, a corporal was delegated to take MacPherson to appear before a local magistrate in Braemar. He set off with a handful of men and the prisoner, but before they could get to the magistrate's house they found themselves surrounded by a mob of clearly unhappy locals.

There was a great deal of shouting, which, although mainly in Gaelic, left the corporal in no doubt of the anger of the people present. Things were beginning to get out of hand so he ordered his men to fix bayonets. At this, the crowd drew slightly back, and the corporal took the opportunity to grab one of them, Allan Coutts, whom he placed under arrest.

The party of soldiers then decided to head back to Braemar Castle with their two prisoners. As they set off, they were approached by a gentleman called Shaw, who they knew was a man of some standing in the area.

'Now then, Corporal,' said Shaw, 'this is an unfortunate situation. If you don't mind, I would like to come along with you and speak to the captain.'

Realising that Shaw's presence might help calm things down, the corporal agreed, and the whole party headed off to the castle. When they got there Shaw told Desclouseaux that he was willing to stand guarantor for Coutts.

'That is all very well, Mr Shaw,' replied Desclouseaux, 'but from what my corporal has told me this man Coutts was actively trying to stop him in the execution of his duty. I have no choice but to bring him before the local justice of the peace and charge him with rioting.'

'If that is what you feel you must do, Captain,' said Shaw with a nod of his head.

So Ensign Butler, the corporal and four soldiers took Coutts off to the local justice of the peace, Mr Gordon. Shaw went along with them. After hearing what the corporal had to say, Gordon had a brief conversation in Gaelic with Shaw, and Butler was astonished to be told that Gordon did not consider himself qualified to rule on the matter. At that point, Shaw said to Gordon in English, 'Well, if you want to bail him in the meantime, I will gladly stand guarantee for him.'

To Butler's astonishment, Gordon agreed at once and Coutts went off with Shaw. A few days later, both MacPherson and Coutts were taken in front of Justice Leith, who had come to Braemar. Because of his age and infirmity, MacPherson was let off with a warning. After the corporal gave his evidence against Coutts, several witnesses were called in his defence and the judge dismissed the case against him. Desclouseaux was furious, and in a letter to his superiors he told them that he had discovered that Coutts was Shaw's servant and that it had been Shaw himself who had stirred up the crowd against the corporal and his party. He said of the local population, 'this is a nest of rogues and rebels.'

The resentment of the locals against the soldiers billeted on them was shown in a letter to Desclouseaux from the Spittal of Glenshee, eleven miles south of Braemar, where a smaller garrison was located. It read: 'I, James McNabb, do absolutely refuse to furnish the detachment of one sergeant and six private men, now quartered in the Spittal of Glenshee with any more firing [firewood] from this day forward. James MacNabb, Constable'.

In August of the same year, Desclouseaux had some success when he managed to arrest eight men sleeping in a cave in the hills who were dressed in Highland garb and carrying arms. They, too, were taken before Judge Leith and charged with breaking the terms of the Disarming Act. However, only three of them were imprisoned; the rest were released on condition of good behaviour. It seems that even the loyal officers of the law, local constables, justices of the peace and judges, had some sympathy with the population of the Highlands about the treatment meted out to them by the Government!

PRINCE CHARLIE

Betty Burke

———⟫◆⟪———

In the summer of 1746 the British Government were in hot pursuit of Prince Charlie. They knew that he was somewhere in the west of Scotland and that, in order to get out of the country, he would be looking to travel by ship to France. This meant that they were both keeping an eye on people travelling out to the Hebrides and patrolling the seacoast north of Argyll with men-o'-war. Argyll being loyal Campbell country the hunt was focused north of there. Now, the prince had many loyal followers, and even the phenomenal reward of thirty thousand pounds for information leading to his capture did not seem to be helping. This was an actual fortune when one thinks that a farm worker's wages were in the region of twenty to twenty-five pounds a year. In the Highlands, of course, money was scarce and most people lived by self-sufficiency farming, making the attraction of the money, if anything, even greater.

The prince had gone out to Uist with Captain O'Neill not long after Culloden, hoping that a ship would come from France. There, he was looked after by various members of the MacDonald clan. By the end of May no ship had arrived and rumours had started circulating that there was to be a great sweep of the Long Island, the name given to the archipelago of North and South Uist, the conjoined islands of Lewis and Harris to the north, and the many smaller islands around them. It was clearly time for Charlie to move elsewhere, and the general consensus amongst his hosts was that he should go to Skye. At that point Flora Mac-Donald arrived on the island, supposedly visiting her brother at Milton. Her stepfather was High MacDonald of Castleton, who happened to be the commander of the Government militia in the Isles. However, she was also acting as a messenger for Lady Margaret MacDonald of Mogstadt on Skye, who was active in trying to organise the prince's escape. While she was on Uist she met Captain O'Neill, who saw in the petite young woman the perfect cover for getting the prince off the island under the noses of his hunters. Having already been accosted by members of the militia and insisting on being taken before their commander, her stepfather, she was above suspicion. Such was the level of security that in order to travel between the islands it was necessary to apply for passports. There were many who didn't and travelled the wild waters of the Minch by night, but they risked their liberty and their lives. It would be much better to travel as openly as possible.

So Flora applied to her stepfather for passports for herself, a young student called Neil MacEachan and a maid called Betty Burke, which were soon forthcoming. Now, it is the way of things with the aristocracy and the rich in general that servants are virtually beneath their notice, and when Flora told him that this Irish lass was a great spinner he thought no more of her, other than to mention in a letter to his wife on Skye that she might find the young lass's skills of some use! It is just as well she never tried to get Betty Burke to spin for her. Flora's party was rowed from Uist to Skye overnight on the 28 June. As they were approaching the coast near Waternish, shortly after dawn, they saw a group of soldiers on the headland and veered off round the point. The soldiers fired some shots after them but no one was hit. Out in the Minch they could see several men-o'-war so they slipped into one of the many creeks on that part of the Skye coast. They spent the whole morning moving slowly and carefully along the coast landing about noon by the mouth of the *Allt a Chuain* burn half a mile from Mogstadt House.

At once, Flora sent the boatmen back to Uist and set off for the house to see Lady MacDonald, telling the prince to keep hidden nearby. She got to the house to find it over-run with army officers, including General Campbell, and had to use all her charm and wits to deflect their questions. Despite the presence of so many officers, she managed to let Lady Margaret know what was happening. Soon after that, MacDonald of Kingsborough, who served as factor for Sir Alexander MacDonald, the chief of the Skye MacDonalds, said he had to go off to attend to some business on the estate. The officers thought nothing of it, and a little while later Kingsborough brought much-needed food and drink to the prince down by the shore.

The prince was, of course, in disguise as Betty Burke, the Irish maid, at this time, and Kingsborough had to remind him to try to remember that he was, for the moment at least, supposed to be a female and to be careful how he carried himself. After Charles had eaten, they set off for Kingsborough's home. On the way, they were noticed by a local man herding some cattle. A day or so later, in a nearby inn, he was sitting with some other locals when someone mentioned MacDonald of Kingsborough and the Irish maid.

'Maid?' he said in a questioning tone of voice. 'A maid is she? Well, I will tell you, and may the Good Lord preserve me if I lie, I saw the woman and there she was striding across the field below the dun with a long stick in her hand and some kind of hood I have never seen before on her head. I tell you, she was dressed very strangely indeed. In fact, if she hadn't been with Kingsborough himself, I would have thought her to be one of those poor unfortunates who the fairies have long had locked up inside the dun and who had just escaped. I never saw a human female like that in all my life and I was glad indeed that she didn't come my way.'

Kingsborough, perfectly aware of how unfeminine Betty Burk was, soon had Prince Charles back in men's attire, and he sent him off with MacEachan to the isle of Raasay, where he lived for a few days in a sheiling, a simple, if not crude, dwelling used by those looking after cattle or sheep. The disguise had served to get him off Uist, but a bonny lassie he was not!

Lewie Caw

⟫⟪

After his stay on the island of Raasay, Prince Charles returned to Skye. For his own safety, he was travelling with just one companion, Malcolm MacLeod, who had held the rank of captain amongst the MacKinnons. The pair of them were making their way to Elgol, MacLeod's home on the Strathaird peninsula on Skye. As they headed on foot towards MacLeod's home they seemed to be just a couple of mud-splattered travellers, who had obviously recently been in contact with a peat bog on their travels. One of them was well dressed and the other, clad in simple hodden grey, the standard dress of Lowland men, with a white 'kerchief tied over his head below his bonnet, was carrying a large case on his shoulders. This was Lewie Caw, the name the prince had taken as part of his disguise as MacLeod's servant. At least it was better than trying to pretend to be Betty Burke! Near Kilmaree they caught up with two men on the road ahead of them. These were a couple of MacKinnons, likewise returning home from that dreadful slaughter on Drumossie Moor. They greeted MacLeod and looked at his companion.

At once, both fell to one knee. They had seen the prince often enough over the previous year to recognise him despite his disguise.

'Get up you fools,' hissed MacLeod. 'If anyone is watching they will know who is with us.'

At once, the two Highlanders jumped to their feet, blushing with embarrassment.

'Now,' MacLeod went on in a stern voice, 'you know that the Hanoverians are searching for him, and I must ask you to swear that you will say nothing to anyone of this meeting. Swear on your dirks.'

This was a serious request. When a Highlander swore on his dirk it was the most solemn oath he could take, much more binding even than swearing on the bible. Effectively, the oath was that if the word was broken the perpetrator forsook all hope of heaven and would give himself over to the Devil himself. It was an ancient oath, possibly based on something similar from pre-Christian times, and any man who broke such an oath would be regarded as an outlaw by all of Highland society and fair game for any who met him. Realising the seriousness of the situation, the two MacKinnon lads immediately whipped out their dirks and gave the oath, finishing by kissing the naked steel of the blades. MacLeod was satisfied. He knew these men well and had no doubt that they would never break such an oath, no matter what might happen to them at the hands of their enemies.

'Fine then,' said MacLeod, 'now stay here with His Majesty till I return. I must spy out the land.' And, nodding to the prince, he headed off further down the road to the house of John Mac-Kinnon, his brother in law. He was well aware that the Royal Navy had ships in the area and that it was possible, perhaps even likely, that troops had been landed in this part of Skye to seek out the prince. Approaching the house cautiously, he went in and let his sister know he had come to hide out for a while with his manservant.

He then headed back and brought his man, still carrying the case, back to the house. The two MacKinnons made their fare-wells and left.

Preparing food for the pair of them, Mrs MacKinnon told

Lewie Caw to sit at the table. At first, he was reluctant but she said, 'Och, dinnae be daft. We stand on no ceremony here. You have come a long way and I am sure you need a good meal. Just sit you down and eat.' This was said in a kindly tone for, as she told her brother later, she had taken to the young manservant right away. What she said was, 'There was something about him.' Now, the pair of them had been on the road and were not only tired and hungry but covered in muck and glaur. MacLeod politely asked the young lass who was acting as a maid to his sister if she would wash his legs and feet, which were absolutely caked with mud. This the young lass was quite happy to do, but when he asked that she perform the same service for his companion the young lass took offence saying, 'What I will do for the master I will not do for the servant. He is nothing but some son of a low-country Sassanach I'll bet. Wash his feet? I certainly will not.' As ever, once Highland pride was pricked the stubborn side of the Highland character came to the fore.

'Och, come on now. You know we have been on the road a good long while and you can see that he is as tired out as I am. It would be a great Christian kindness you would be doing for the poor lad,' MacLeod pleaded. At first, she would have none of it, but calling on her sympathy MacLeod eventually convinced her to wash Prince Charlie's legs and feet. She set to the task, though with an ill will and a great deal of sighing and grunting. She was a strong young woman and within a couple of minutes Lewie had to ask her to take things easy as she was carrying out the task with just a bit too much enthusiasm! Noticing how agitated her brother was throughout this episode, Mrs MacKinnon began to put two and two together. When MacLeod told Lewie to get some sleep she looked at her brother and smiled. Charles went into a bedroom and fell across the bed, fully dressed in his stained clothing. At once he was asleep.

While he slept, the faithful MacLeod and his sister kept watch. Some time later Mrs MacKinnon went outside. She knew her husband would be coming soon, he had returned home a few days earlier from the campaign, and she wanted to stop him before he entered the house. He, too, had met the prince, and she realised it was important not to let the maid and the others around the place realise just who it was they had staying with them. With the thirty-thousand-pound reward on the prince's head, it was advisable to take as many precautions as possible. So MacKinnon came home to be met on the road a little distance from his house by his wife, who informed him that Prince Charles Edward Stewart was in their house, and when he came in to find the prince, clad in little more than rags, and dandling the youngest of the MacKinnon laddies on his knee, the poor man couldn't stop himself bursting into tears.

Soon, however, Charles's famous way with people had calmed him down, and the discussion turned to finding a boat to take the prince off Skye. MacLeod stated that the best thing would be to return to the mainland and soon MacKinnon, sworn to secrecy, went off to find a boat. However, as he left the house he met Iain Dubh, the MacKinnon himself, and at once told his chief the situation. Secrecy was one thing but telling the chief was the right thing to do. So it was that the chief of the MacKinnons took it on himself to organise matters. Meanwhile, MacLeod, worried that word might get out, took the refreshed Charlie, still in his servant's clothes, to wait in a cave near the point at Elgol until the boat could be arranged. This cave has ever since been known to the locals as *Uamh na Phrionnsa*, the Prince's Cave. That same night, 4 July 1746, after a cold meal of meat and bread, the prince left Skye with MacLeod, MacKinnon and four others, never to set foot on the island again. As for the lass in the kitchen, when she was told later whose feet she had handled so roughly she was quite upset. But only for a little while for, with the resilience of youth, she soon realised that she had a grand story to tell her own children and grandchildren in the fullness of time.

Prince Charlie and the milk pail

⟹◆⟸

Only months after the great day of the Raising of the Standard at Glenfinnan things had changed remarkably. In 1746 Prince Charlie was hiding out in the hills above Glenaladale, just south-west of Glenfinnan, and he must have looked back ruefully to that day when all things had seemed possible. Now he was a fugitive, hunted by the red-coated soldiers and with the fantastic sum of thirty thousand pounds on his head. He was hiding in a cave with Alexander MacDonald of Glenaladale, and waiting for word from Donald Cameron of Glen Spean as to when it would be safe to move. There were just the two of them, little food, no drink and certainly none of the luxuries to which he had become accustomed throughout his life on the Continent. Comparisons with the splendour of life at the Court at St Germain, with its balls, beautiful women, soft beds, hot baths and servants to do his bidding at every hand, must have crossed his mind. Now, here he was, wearing the same clothes he had had on for weeks, hungry, unwashed and thoroughly uncomfortable in a hole in a mountainside looking over what was little more than wilderness.

He was sitting there thinking of what might have been when Glenaladale whispered, 'Listen, there is someone coming.'

Carefully, Glenaladale looked out of the mouth of the cave, a loaded and cocked pistol in his hand. There, coming up the slope to the cave, was a woman. He recognised her as Mhairi MacDonald from the glen below, who had helped look after him when he was a child.

She looked up as she approached the cave and saw him.

With smile she said, 'Ach, it is yourself. I had heard that you were here and I have brought you a pail of fresh milk and some new-made bannocks. It is not much but it is all we can spare.'

As she said this she was looking beyond her chief at the bedraggled figure behind him. On hearing her approach, Prince Charlie had taken his dirty handkerchief and tied it round his head as if he was suffering from toothache. This, he hoped, would prevent anyone recognising him. By now he knew there was a bounty of thirty thousand pounds on his head, and he had received word a week before that a rumour was going round that the Government had been circulating miniature portraits of him throughout the western Highlands. She sniffed and shifted her gaze back to Glenaladale, clearly unimpressed by the stranger.

'Here,' she said, offering the pail. 'Drink all you can, Glenaladale, and let your companion have the rest. I'll be needing the *goganan* for it is the only one I have now since the red-coated swine came through the glen.'

Glenaladale took the pail, saying thank you as he did so. He found himself in a bit of a dilemma. He did not want to offend the prince by drinking before offering him the pail of milk. But if he didn't do so Mhairi would realise that this was a high-ranking stranger, and all she would have to do was put two and two together to realise just who it was. While Alexander was sure of her loyalty he did not want to put her to the test. She had always had a bit of a reputation for enjoying gossip, and if she told others who was hiding in the hills the situation could deteriorate rapidly.

'Ach, that's grand,' he said. 'Why don't you just leave us the pail and come back for it later?'

'Well, I'll be needing it for the evening milking,' she replied.

'Och, I am sure you can always borrow another one. And I tell you what, I will make sure that you get this one back and I'll add in five silver shillings once things have calmed down,' Glenaladale said to her.

Now, Mhairi was not the kind of woman to be deflected from her purpose but this was Glenaladale himself and she knew he would keep his word. She stood looking at him for a minute and then glanced again at his companion. The look on her eye clearly suggested that, though she might be prepared to trust her chief, there was no way she would put her faith in this bedraggled and suspicious looking character.

'Och, come on now,' said Glenaladale, 'it's not that much to ask is it? It's just that we have both had a drink of water a little while ago and it would be better if we could save some of the milk for later on.'

'Hmmm,' the woman mused. 'I suppose it's all right. You'll not be leaving that one there with my *goganan* though will you?' she asked, pointing her finger accusingly at Prince Charles Edward Stewart.

'Ah no,' replied Glenaladale, biting his lip. 'I can assure you he and I will be together all the time till we leave the glen. But,' he added hurriedly, 'I will make sure that you get your *goganan* back if you don't come for it yourself tomorrow.'

'Ach, all right,' sniffed Mhairi, 'I'll come back again tomorrow, with some more bannocks too, but mind and look after thon *goganan*. I wish you well, Sir.'

It was with a great sense of relief that the two men saw this kind-hearted and loyal woman head back down to the clachan at Glenaladale, and once she was out of sight the pair of them burst into laughter. It wasn't till several weeks later that Mhairi found out just who Glenaladale's companion had been, but she was woman enough to see the humour in the situation and for many years after was glad to tell the tale of how she was reluctant to trust Prince Charles Edward Stewart with her valuable milk pail.

JACOBITE GOLD

Prince Charlie's pilots

About the end of July 1745 a ship was spotted anchored off the shore of Eilean Olamsay, just off Colonsay, the small island that lies a few miles west of the long island of Jura and opposite the notorious Corryvreckan whirlpool. It was clearly not a British ship, and the population of the island were somewhat curious. Their curiosity only increased when a small boat came ashore and a couple of well-dressed gentlemen alighted and went to visit Donald MacNeill, the chief of the Colonsay MacNeills. Donald was taken aback to find out that the two men had come directly from Prince Charles Edward Stewart aboard the ship. They wanted to know if he would give his support to the attempt to overthrow the Hanoverians and reinstall the Stewarts as the kings of Great Britain. They also told him that they intended landing a considerable sum of gold coin, which was to be used to help their cause. They were hoping that this could be safely hidden on Colonsay, under MacNeill's protection, till it was needed.

MacNeill wanted nothing to do with the endeavour and told them so in very clear terms. When the boat returned with this message, Prince Charles himself came ashore and visited MacNeill at Kiloran to try to persuade him to help. Despite the prince's undoubted charm, MacNeill was adamant. Although he would not inform the authorities of the prince's presence, he wanted no part in any rebellion. He also said that if they wanted to hide their gold Colonsay was too small an island. The chief's brother, Archibald, went so far as to say that the MacNeills were close supporters of Clan Campbell and, as such, were staunch Hanoverians. The prince and his companions were taken aback: they had expected that all the clans apart from the Campbells would be supportive of their cause. There was also, it would appear, a hint that some of the gold might find its way into the pockets of the MacNeills, but they scorned the offer. Realising that they would get nowhere with the MacNeills, the prince then asked if he could be provided with a couple of local men to serve as pilots, as his crew were ignorant of the waters of the Inner Hebrides. He could then get off Colonsay and land on the mainland. There were many reefs and small islands between them and the mainland, the currents were strong and without good local knowledge trying to land would be taking a consider-able risk. They had probably heard of the dangerous whirlpool of the Corryvreckan between the islands of Scarba and Jura and had no wish to end up in its grip. MacNeill was in no mood to help and refused point blank. There was little that the prince and his company could do. In fact, they were lucky that MacNeill did not decide to take them prisoner there and then, capturing their ship and the casks containing the gold.

By this time word had gone around the island that the prince had landed and was needing a couple of pilots. None of the MacNeills were prepared to go against their chief, but two brothers, Iain and Hector MacMillan, were interested. After talking it over for a while, they rowed out to the ship to say that they would do the job. However, they said they would do it for pay, and each demanded one of the small kegs of gold coin the ship was carrying for his service. This was an exorbitant demand and effectively extortion, but they had the Jacobites at their mercy. The longer the Jacobites stayed where they were the more likely they were to be discovered by one of the ships of the Royal Navy. There was also the added possibility that MacNeill would decide to take some decisive action against them.

Prince Charlie himself said that he would give them a keg of gold each, once they had landed him and his party on the mainland, but the brothers were adamant. They wanted paying in advance. So it was that the two brothers were given a keg of gold apiece. By himself, Iain took the gold ashore in their boat and handed the kegs over to a family member for safekeeping. Hector remained on board the ship. Iain then returned to join his brother. By this time night was beginning to fall, and it was decided that it would be better to wait till morning before setting sail. The two brothers bedded down aboard the ship, but in the middle of the night Hector, the younger of the two, awoke. Lying in the gently rocking ship, he began to have second thoughts about this whole affair. The more he thought about it, the less he liked the idea of becoming involved in this dangerous enterprise. If he were caught he would be charged with treason. He had no particular sympathies for the Jacobite cause and decided that, whatever he was being paid, risking his life was not a good idea. So, without even waking his brother, he slipped gently over the side and swam ashore. He did not give more than a passing thought to returning the gold. In the morning his absence was noted and Iain was dragged before the prince.

'Well, MacMillan,' Prince Charles asked through an interpreter, 'where is your brother?'

'I am sorry, Your Highness,' came the reply, 'but if he is not on board the ship then you know as much as I.'

'Is it common for people of your kin to take advance payment for work they have no intention of performing?' the prince asked in a cold voice.

Now, clansmen were famous for taking great pride in their sense of honour, and this was the kind of question that would usually send them into a fury. Iain, though, realised that Hector's actions were shameful and, swallowing his pride, he replied.

'No, Your Highness, it is not, and I can only apologise for the dishonourable behaviour of my brother. I will fulfil the terms of our agreement to the very best of my ability and I will swear that on my dirk.'

He was as good as his word. That day he safely piloted the ship to the mainland and the rest of the gold was unloaded. However, once that was done, and as Prince Charlie and his advisers made ready to go ashore themselves, Iain approached them.

'Your Highness,' he said, 'I beg your pardon but, if you will allow it, I would like to come with you. I can fight with sword and gun, and I would consider it an honour to be amongst your forces.'

Whether he had fallen under the influence of the charismatic Young Pretender, or whether he was set on removing the blot on his family's honour caused by his brother's cowardly desertion is unclear, but his actions were decisive. His offer was, of course, accepted and Iain MacMillan accompanied the Jacobite army all through the ensuing campaign.

He stayed close to the prince, and when, after his long months in the heather, Charles Edward Stewart at last boarded the French ship *L'Heureux* to sail to France he was accompanied by Iain as pilot. Once he found himself in France, Iain found that he got on well with the locals and decided to settle there. Within a few years he was happily married, and though he kept in touch with his relatives in Colonsay he never returned to reclaim his own keg of gold. As for his brother, Hector used his gold wisely and prospered on Colonsay. The Colonsay MacNeills did not come out for Charlie, but in 1746 when the Government was gathering as many men as it could to finish off the rebellion it was notable that they were in fact unable to recruit any men from among the Colonsay MacNeills, despite the influence of MacCalien Mor, the Campbell Duke of Argyll.

Gold in the Great Chanter

The kegs of gold that Colonsay people say were hidden by Hector MacMillan are not the only instance of Jacobite gold disappearing. On the west coast of Sutherland there was a large gully known as *Am Feodan Mor*, the Great Chanter, and it too had its story of hidden gold. The tale goes that one Duncan Macrae was given the care of a hogshead of gold to look after in the months after Culloden. Gold was always needed to pay for soldiers and to feed and arm them. Now, a hogshead was a wooden barrel that held seventy-two gallons of liquid, so the amount of gold must have been considerable. Duncan was a man known to have the second sight, but he was also possessed of other powers. It was well known in the Highlands that not only women had the power of magic, and in truth Duncan was thought of as being a bit of a wizard or magician. This made him the ideal man to hide the gold that might well be needed if and when the prince returned to Scotland. So he and couple of companions carried the gold to *Am Feodan Mor*, and there it was buried with all the necessary spells and incantations that Duncan knew. They then left it hidden there, sure that no one would ever find it unless they knew the secret of Duncan's spell. And a strange spell it was for the spell he had put on the hogshead meant that the hogshead could only be seen once every seven years on the very day that it had been buried.

The secret was told only to a few, and as the years passed and Prince Charles did not return to the Scottish Highlands the secret was itself lost. This had a lot to do with the way the clanspeople were driven out of many parts of the Highlands in the years after Culloden and, sporadically, ever since. Those that left and knew the secret, like so many others, never returned. And if Duncan Macrae and Prince Charlie's gold was ever mentioned among those that stayed, well, 'It was just a story, wasn't it?' was what was said.

Now, the area where the gold had been buried was deserted in 1746, but by the time a hundred years had passed a *tigh dubh* or black house had been built at the top of the gully, where a croft had been carved out of the rough moorland. Many of the people from more fertile parts of the Highlands had been driven to farm and fish along the shores as the Clearances gathered pace and sheep and deer took over the glens and straths. There, at the top of the gully one fine summer's evening in 1844, ninety-eight years to the day after the gold had been buried, the goodwife of the croft was sitting at her door spinning wool. She was spinning away, gently crooning an old lullaby, when she looked down the slope, and there jutting from the ground was the top of a wooden cask. She looked at it, puzzled, for a moment. Then all at once she remembered the story her great-grandmother had told her, when she was just a few years old, of Duncan MacRae and Prince Charlie's gold. Prince Charlie had never come back and the gold would belong to whoever found it – once the Government took its cut of course. Realising that she could never get the gold out of the ground herself – her man was off fishing at the time – she wondered what to do. If she couldn't get it out of the ground before nightfall it would disappear for another seven years!

Then it came to her what she had to do. There was plenty gold there for more than just her, her man and her three wee toddlers. She could well afford to go and fetch help to get the great barrel out of the ground. Then, clambering down to where the barrel jutted from the earth, she stuck her distaff in the ground alongside the hogshead of gold. Scrambling back up the slope, she dressed her children in their best clothes, picked up the littlest and the three of them headed off to the nearest village, about five miles off, to get help. By the time she reached the village the gloaming was well advanced and it was clear that there was no way of getting aback to *Am Feodan Mor* before nightfall. So she sat up late that night with her relatives in the village, all excited about the discovery of the gold. Many glasses of peatreek, locally made whisky on which no duty would ever be paid, were drunk to toast Prince Charlie and his treasure and the goodwife for her presence of mind in marking the gold's location before it disappeared again. There was many a bleary eye the following morning when a large group of villagers accompanied her back to the croft.

As they approached the rim of the great gorge hearts were a-fluttering with excitement. Truth to tell there was no one there who didn't have a hard time of it, and the thought of all the riches to some cleared many heads! They came to the croft house and passed it. As they all stood along the lip of the chasm and looked down it was obvious to them all just what had happened. For there was no sign at all of where the good wife had planted her distaff. Such was the power of Duncan MacRae's spell that when it had returned to hide the hogshead once more it also hid the distaff. Try as they might, not one of them could find a thing, and it was sad and tired crowd of villagers who returned home that day. As for the goodwife, by the time the next seven years had passed she had half a dozen bairns to tend to, and she and her husband had moved off to one of the cities in the south of the country. Not everybody has forgotten all about Prince Charlie's gold though, and if only you knew the day that it reappears you might just find it yourself.

Duncan the Seeker

⟹◆⟸

In the years at the beginning of the eighteenth century there was a great deal of contact between Jacobites in both Scotland and England and those on the Continent, particularly in the period immediately before 1715. Ships carrying claret from Bordeaux to the ever-thirsty market in Scotland were often used to transport both arms and money. The British Navy did not have enough ships to monitor every vessel that made its way from France to Britain and many got through. Sometimes, there were considerable amounts of both gold and weapons, but at other times the supplies came in small amounts. Duncan Graham, a Perthshire man, had gone off in the early years of the century to join the Jacobite court in France. Both his parents were dead, he had no brothers or sisters and he was a strong supporter of the cause. He went on to serve in one of the Scottish regiments in the French army till, in November 1715, he was put in charge of a consignment heading to Britain in a small ship with five fellow Scots. The consignment consisted of a fair amount of gold, swords, muskets and gunpowder, all of which was intended to be distributed amongst Jacobite sympathisers in north-west England. Duncan's intention was to land on the southern shore of the Solway Firth and hide the supplies while he made contact with the men whose names he had been given. He would then help them distribute the money and arms before heading north to join up with the rebellion in Scotland.

As he sailed up through the Irish Sea, his ship was spotted by an English cruiser, which immediately gave chase. Luckily, Duncan's ship was considerably faster than the Navy one, but the chase drove him north of his intended landing and by the time they had given the cruiser the slip the ship was sailing up the Firth of Clyde. Now, in those far off times news took time to travel and he was unaware of the current situation of the Jacobite army. He made landfall by night between Helensburgh and Dumbarton and went ashore to find out how things stood, hoping to hear news of a great Jacobite victory.

He made his way to a local tavern and went in to have a drink.

Before leaving France, he had made sure that he was dressed as plainly as possible and no one paid much attention to him in the tavern. As he sat at a table drinking, he heard the story of Mar's debacle at Sheriffmuir and the pathetic surrender at Preston. Clearly, there would be little point in looking to find his contacts in the north-west of England. They were likely to be dead or in prison. From what he had heard, it was clear that Bobbing John, as the locals scathingly referred to Mar, was still at Perth. So, downing his drink, he headed back to the ship. He was in a quandary; from the way the locals had been speaking, some bitterly and others disparagingly, it seemed as if the Rising was effectively over. He also realised that the country between him and Perth was liable to be over-run with red-coated soldiers and the Campbell clansmen of the Duke of Argyll's army. Transporting weapons through the countryside would be foolish, but maybe he could get the money to Mar. It would be useful for another attempt later. At the very least he would have done something positive for the cause if he got the money through.

So he and his five companions unloaded the arms and the money before telling the ship's captain to return to France as best he could. They buried the arms and the barrel full of gold not far from the shore and lay down to sleep, wrapped in the blankets they had brought from the ship. The following day, Duncan made his way to Dumbarton, where he bought a dozen strong leather satchels, then headed back to where his friends were. They then dug up and distributed the gold between the satchels, and, carrying two of them apiece, they headed off through the Lennox, the lands to the east of Loch Lomond. They were armed with pistols and swords and made slow progress because, desperate not to run into any army patrols, they regularly stopped and sent a couple of their number ahead to scout out the land. There were so many troops about that they were forced to head north towards the Trossachs, hoping to make their way to Perth along the southern edge of the mountains.

They managed to buy enough food to keep going as they went, but there seemed to be Government troops everywhere. However, Duncan was not a man to be put off once he had his mind set, and they soldiered on. Three days later, however, they had only got as far as the slopes of Ben Ledi, overlooking Loch Venachar, and it was obvious they could not carry on as they were. They had seen numerous army patrols over the previous twenty-four hours, and Duncan reluctantly decided they would have to bury the gold, split up and try to get through to Perth one by one. Even if only one of them got through he might be able to return later with enough of a force to reclaim the gold. So, they buried the gold in the shade of a large boulder, ate some of the bread and cheese they had managed to buy that morning and washed it down with water from the nearby burn. They then set off east, intending to split up within the hour. What they didn't know was that the man who had sold them the bread and cheese that morning had sent word to the local garrison that there was a group of suspicious strangers heading east. They had only gone half an hour from where the gold was buried when they heard a cry from behind them:

'Stand, in the king's name!'

They turned to see twenty soldiers coming down the shoulder of the hill they had just crossed. They were severely outnumbered but Duncan hardly noticed. All of his disappointment and tiredness disappeared as a wave of rage and hatred against the soldiers swept over him. He turned, whipped out his pistols and fired at the oncoming soldiers. One of them fell, and as Duncan's companions began to fire the soldiers fired a volley back at them. Then, before he could think, Duncan, sword in hand, was lunging at a large red-faced soldier whose face was as set in hatred as his own. The soldier tried to parry Duncan's lunge, but the sword pierced his side just as one of his fellows caught Duncan's shoulder with his bayonet. Duncan hardly noticed as he swung at the two more Redcoats who were coming at him. The battle, though, was short. Outnumbered as they were, there was little hope for Duncan's party. Duncan, himself, was finally hacked down from behind by the officer in charge, having already sustained a number of serious wounds. As he crashed to the heather, covered in blood, his companions threw down their weapons. They were outmatched. To fight on would be to die, and for what? The soldiers tied their arms behind their backs and marched them off, leaving the body of Duncan Graham lying in the heather.

It was late that day when a band of Highlanders, MacIntyres, who had been off taking cattle to market and were heading towards Strathyre, came upon the body lying in the heather. They had not been in Mar's army, but their sympathy was with the Stewarts rather than the Hanoverians. And they realised that this man had been fighting with the soldiers they had seen at a distance earlier that day. They had been escorting some prisoners and it seemed likely that this man had been one of the their party. The man in the front of the group, a stocky, dark-haired and bearded man, dressed, like his companions, in the Highland plaid, knelt down and felt at Duncan's neck for a pulse. It was faint but the man was still alive, if only just.

'Right, lads, lets see to his wounds and we'll carry him with us,' he said, adding, 'Those German-loving swine didn't even check to see if he was dead.'

They carried him to a cottage not far off where one of their kin lived and left him there to recover. Nursed by the lady of the house, for days it seemed as if he would not recover as he thrashed about in a fever, his wounds bursting open anew.

It was fully a week before he opened his eyes to find himself inside a black house with a fair-haired woman standing over him with a bowl in her hands.

'Here,' she said, 'I will help you take some of this broth.'

So saying, she put the bowl on the edge of the bed and, gently lifting his head, gave him small sips of the liquid from a horn spoon. After only a few sips of the venison broth Duncan fell back and once more drifted into sleep, but this time he was more peaceful.

Over the next few months, he gradually regained his strength, but he seemed confused. He told his hosts his name but little else, every question meeting with the reply that he was in charge of the king's gold. His mind had clearly been affected by what had happened and, even as he grew stronger, it became clear that he was brain damaged. By the time he was able to walk again many months had passed, and the MacIntyres and their neighbours all knew well that he was obsessed with one idea and one idea alone. He said he had to go and get the king's gold for the Earl of Mar. The MacIntyres tried to look after him, but once he was fit and well they could not keep him any more. He rose one morning and left to look for the buried gold.

However strong his sense of duty, however committed he was

to the cause, however much he wanted to fulfil his mission he simply could not. He could remember burying the gold and little else after it. He knew he had been in a fight that nearly killed him, but all that remained of the incident were a few blurred impressions. The damage to his memory was such that he could not remember where he had buried the gold. His companions had been either killed or transported and he was the only one left. He was a man obsessed, walking endlessly round the slopes of Ben Ledi and further afield looking for anything that might remind him of where he had left the king's gold. The local people became used to him on his travels, and, as he was clearly damaged, all took turns to feed him and give him clothes when he needed them.

For many years after the '15 he was to be seen haunting the area, muttering constantly to himself, 'I must find the gold, the Earl needs it,' unaware that Bobbing John had long since fled the country. The people in the area came to call him Duncan the Seeker, and it was many years later that one of the sons of the MacIntyres who had looked after him found his body lying in the heather on the hill. He had lost the gold but never his loyalty to the cause.

LOYALTY TO THE CAUSE

Donald of Kinloch

⪡◆⪢

Donald MacDonald of Kinlochmoidart, chief of the Clanranald MacDonalds, generally known as Donald of Kinloch, was with Prince Charlie from the start. He was widely reckoned to be a fine example of a Highland warrior chief, brave, loyal and honourable. In the years before the prince arrived he had been actively involved in contacts between France and the loyal clans and had shown a cool head in several difficult situations. Within days of his gallant behaviour at Rose Castle, which he had put under his protection, he was sent northwards by Charles to Edinburgh on a mission of some importance. Sadly, however, the whole of Scotland had not been secured when the Jacobite army marched south, and he was recognised in the capital by a man who had been a tutor to him and his brothers in their youth. Either this gentleman was a staunch Hanoverian or he let it slip who Kinloch was. The upshot of it was that, travelling with only one companion, he was easily taken prisoner and carried off to Edinburgh Castle, which remained in Government hands throughout the whole of the Rising.

After the retreat from Derby, the Governor of Edinburgh Castle sent Kinloch to Carlisle where, along with other captured Jacobites, he was to stand trial. Among the prisoners were several of his own close kin including Donald MacDonell of Tirnadris, the hero of the Battle of High Bridge, who had been captured at Falkirk after having fought his way too far into the enemy's lines to be able to escape.

189

When Kinloch was tried the following autumn there was never any doubt as to what his sentence would be. Like most of the trials of the time, it was little more than a pretence; for his crimes in plotting against the Government and then coming out in arms against the Hanoverians he could only be sentenced to death. And not just death, but the full sentence for treason: death by being hung, drawn and quartered. Back on the shores of Loch Moidart, in the shadow of Creag Liath Behag, his old mother was forced to watch from the shade of a copse of yew trees while Kinlochmoidart House was burned to the ground by the Redcoats. It was too much for the old woman, and as the ashes cooled to grey she drew her last breath. Donald's wife fled to the hills with her wee bairns and despite attempts by various clansmen to help her, she lost her mind.

Back in Carlisle, Donald took the news bitterly but never let it show to his captors. He had gambled and failed, though he had never thought that his family would be forced to suffer as they had at the hands of a revenge-seeking British Government. Like many of the Highland clansmen, he was a Catholic, and he wished to have communion and give his last confession before going to his death. There was no chance, however, that the Hanoverian troops would allow him a priest in to give him his final rites. Still, he felt he must try. Just as today there are few, if any, prisons that are totally secure, it wasn't too hard for MacDonald to get word out to Bishop Smith in Edinburgh asking him to send a priest to give him communion before he was executed. This would clearly need a man of cool temperament and considerable courage for, if his true purpose was discovered, a priest entering the jail would soon become one of its inmates! Luckily, the right man was to hand. This was Father George Duncan, a man who had for a while been in charge of the small Catholic seminary in Loch Morar and who was in fact a good friend of Kinloch's. On being told of the request, he set off almost at once to Carlisle. He passed himself off as a relative of Kinloch's and was allowed in to see him. Mac-Donald's companions did not even realise who had come amongst them and, when left alone with Kinloch, the priest was able to give his friend confession and Holy Communion. He then took a sad farewell of his friend before heading back north. Somehow, though, word of his mission got out soon after, and he was not long on the road when a group of dragoons was sent after him. Duncan, however, managed to give them the slip and headed back north, where he was soon in hiding amongst his faithful congregation.

On 18 October MacDonald's sentence was carried out in public view. All the barbarity of English law came into force as he was first hung, until he was half dead, then cut down and disembowelled, and his bowels set on fire while he still drew breath. Then, once life was extinct, his head was struck off and placed on a spike over one of the gates in the defensive wall of Carlisle. His companion, Tirnadris, was likewise treated with all the respect of the law. For many years Kinloch's skull sat above the gate, and it was soon noted that no one of Highland birth, and many another Scot, would pass through that gate without saluting the skull bleaching slowly in the wind, rain and sun.

A few years later, Allan MacDonald, a native of Glenuig in Moidart, was brought before the Governor of the castle. His crime was that in full public view he had climbed up the gate and kissed the skull of his former clan chief, where once his lips had been. Such was the affection that could flourish within the Highland clans that even death would not stop him showing his true feelings to a man he had so loved and admired. By this time, the country was becoming more settled and the chance of another rebellion seemed to be growing less. The Governor, a Scot himself, from the Lennox area, realised that there would be no great advantage in making an example of Allan and released him with an admonishment. His actions had clearly been supportive of the recent rebellion, but the governor thought tact preferential to brutality. In fact, he was so touched by the devotion shown by Allan that within days the head of Donald MacDonald of Kinlochmoidart was taken down from the spike on which it had sat and quietly and decently buried.

Born to the cause

⟫◆⟪

After the fiasco of the Rising of 1715 many leading Jacobites fled abroad, and others were forced into hiding in Scotland. One of these was Sir David Thriepland of Fingask Castle, a few miles east of Perth, at the foot of the Sidlaws, or Seedlie Hills. By spring 1716, the Jacobites were in total disarray, and David was pretty sure that Fingask Castle would soon be occupied by Government troops. James Stewart, the Old Pretender, or King James III of England and VIII of Scotland as the Jacobites referred to him, had stayed at Fingask on 8 January on his way to Perth. In less than a month he had fled Scotland, having failed to rally enough support to make any difference to the already hopeless situation. He had also greatly disappointed his loyal followers, and, soon after, the Jacobite army disbanded at Ruthven in Strathspey, the Highland clansmen disappearing back to their own homes. The pursuing Government troops did not have to fire a shot.

The attempt at bringing back the Stewarts had been an utter failure, and to all intents and purposes the whole of Scotland was under the control of the Hanoverian Government. Despite being on the run, Thriepland was primarily concerned about his wife. She was heavily pregnant at the time, and he decided to remain in the area, hiding out in one of the houses on the Fingask estate. He was helped by David Ritchie, who had been working for his family for years.

There was usually a religious aspect to the Jacobite cause and, though Thriepland was an Episcopalian, Ritchie was himself a Presbyterian. The minister at nearby Kinnaird was, like many of his calling, a staunch Hanoverian, seeing the accession of the House of Hanover to the thrones of England and Scotland as the best possible defence for his own religion – which, of course, he saw as the one true faith – against the papist actions of the Stewarts and their followers.

He accosted Ritchie after service one Sunday.

'Now, David Ritchie, it is your bounden duty as a true Christian to give your support to the church and to the legal king. Do you not agree?' he asked in a stern voice.

'I am not sure what you are getting at, Minister,' replied Ritchie, knowing fine well what the man was about.

'It has come to my attention that David Thriepland is skulking in the area. He is a condemned rebel and a supporter of the papist Stewarts, and it is your duty to tell me where he is so I can inform the authorities,' the minister went on with all the authority he could muster. 'I am well aware that he could hardly be hiding out without your knowledge, Sir, so tell me where he is,' he demanded.

'I am sorry, Minister. That is something I cannot do,' replied Ritchie, with a bow of his head.

'I am warning you, David Ritchie, to search your heart and conscience. If you do not do as I ask I will have no choice but to withdraw the sacrament from you,' the minister spluttered, getting angrier by the minute.

Now, today this threat might seem little enough, but in those times being deprived of the sacrament meant that David would not be allowed to attend church and, like many Presbyterians, he was devout man and believed that by missing out on religious observance he would likely be condemning himself to damnation. However, he also knew that, despite the minister's blustering, he was unlikely to implement his threat. There were many people in his congregation who, despite their religious beliefs, still supported the Stewarts against the incoming foreigners of the House of Hanover. The wounds caused by centuries of battle between Scotland and England ran deep, and resentment against the all too recent Act of Union, which had been pushed through by blatant bribery and corruption, was considerable. It was unlikely that the minister would risk alienating a great many of his own congregation.

When his threat failed to move Ritchie the minister dismissed him with the sentence, 'Well, the sin is on your own head, not mine.'

If Ritchie thought this was the last trouble the minister would cause he under-estimated his man. The withdrawal of the sacrament from Ritchie might have been a step too far but the minister wasn't beaten yet. The day after his confrontation with Ritchie he arrived at the great yett, or iron gate, of Fingask Castle, demanding to see Lady Thriepland. On being shown into her presence he wasted no time.

'I have heard news that greatly disturbs me, Your Ladyship. Your husband, the notorious rebel, is nowhere to be found in all the country, yet my parishioners tell me that a strange man has been seen entering the castle late at night on several occasions recently. I must remind you that adultery is a sin in the eyes of the Lord and that if you are a sinner you will undoubtedly be punished for your transgressions.'

Now, given that Lady Catherine Thriepland was six months pregnant at this time, this was quite an accusation but the ways of the devout are probably known only to their gods. He was obviously hoping that Lady Thriepland could be scared into admitting that the strange man seen about the castle grounds was, in fact, her husband. At this point he would inform the

Government and troops would be sent to try to arrest him. Yet again, however, he underestimated his opponent, and Lady Thriepland sweetly replied, 'I am afraid I do not know what you are talking about.'

Both of them knew that this was a blatant lie, but she was not going to give up her husband to imprisonment and possible execution for his role in the Rising. So, the minister was forced to leave Fingask, having got no further in his plan to have Thriepland caught. It was obvious, however, that he was a determined man and that it would be good idea if David Thriepland got out of the area. The minister wasn't the only problem: rewards were being made available to those who would inform on rebels. David realised it was probably only a matter of time before he would be captured and decided he must leave the country.

Once he had made his decision there was no time to waste. After a tearful farewell from his wife, Thriepland headed north. The north-east of Scotland, an area full of Episcopalians, was staunch Jacobite, and he hoped to find a ship in one of the ports there that would take him to the Continent. Despite the debacle of the rebellion, there were still enough people in the country loyal to the Jacobite cause for him to make his way north without being caught. In Burghead he found a ship sailing to France. His nerves were not helped by the fact that the ship went to Caithness and Orkney before heading south. He was constantly troubled with thought of what was happening to his Catherine.

Back at Fingask Lady Catherine was doing the best she could. Only a day or so after her husband had gone, a contingent of dragoons arrived at the castle. Their captain marched straight into the main hall where Catherine was waiting. He nodded politely but his words were blunt.

'You have twenty minutes, My Lady, to gather up your

possessions and leave this place. My men and I are occupying Fingask under specific orders. Do you understand?' he said.

At once, she started giving orders to the servants and pandemonium erupted. Over the next quarter of an hour all sorts of stuff was hidden in the garden, silver plate and candles, valuable silks and even some jewellery. The plan was to come and gather it up later. However, the officer of the dragoons, a captain, had been taken aback at the sight of Lady Catherine. He had not been told she was pregnant. Although not a big woman, Lady Catherine, like some women do, had grown considerably during pregnancy, and to the captain's inexperienced eye she looked as if she was be ready to give birth at any time!

When the twenty minutes was almost up he approached the distraught woman again. 'Lady Catherine, I beg your pardon,' he said, taking off his hat, 'I did not realise how tender your condition was. You may stay where you are for the moment at least. My men and I shall sleep here in the hall.' He then gave a curt nod and turned away.

This was great relief to Catherine and, calling on a couple of her maids, she went upstairs to the main bedroom where she fell into bed, totally drained. Meanwhile, the servants went and retrieved the valuables that had been stashed in the garden. She fell into a disturbed sleep but awoke in the middle of the night with only one thought.

The bible, the family bible with all of the details of the Thrieplands over generations was still where it always was, on a table in a small side-room off the main hall. It was not only of great value to the Thrieplands, it was also decorated with gold and just the sort of thing that would attract greedy eyes. And the hall was full of British dragoons, whose reputation was not of the best. In a remarkable display of courage, Catherine rose from her bed and softly, holding a candle above her head, made her way downstairs to the main hall. There, she carefully stepped round the sleeping men to the room where the bible lay, her heart pounding so loud she thought it would waken the troops. At last, she made her way to the room and slowly opened the door, breathing a great sigh of relief that only a week before the squeaking door had been oiled! Once in the room, she grabbed the bible and, clutching it to her breast, made the return journey, expecting every second to hear a shout, or perhaps worse. If any of the dragoons had woken to see an indistinct figure carrying a candle they would not have been likely to waste time in checking who it was. The reaction would be to shoot first and ask any questions later. So it was with the blood pounding in her ears and cold sweat dripping down her back that she at last made it back to her bedroom and fell into bed once more.

Within days the captain's understanding and politeness was seen to have been judicious. A letter came from Lieutenant-General Cadogan, the Commander-in-Chief of the Government forces in Scotland, to let Lady Catherine remain at Fingask. Behind the scenes there had been a great deal of influence peddling and she at least was left with a roof over her head. The Fingask estate, however, was 'attained', or confiscated, by the Government and sold to the York Buildings Company. They, in turn, were happy to lease the castle to Lady Thriepland and she kept her home.

So it was that when she eventually gave birth she was secure in the knowledge she had a home in which to raise her child. She had shown great courage and resilience over the three preceding months, but it had taken its toll. The birth was long and difficult, and the doctor who was called in to help with the birth sent for an Episcopalian minister from Perth to be in attendance. They were not sure if either the baby or his mother would survive for long, and it was important that the wee laddie was baptised before he gave up his life. The doctor, the local women who were in attendance and the minister were all clustered round the bed looking down at the deathly pale face of Lady Catherine and the weak, pathetic-looking son that she had given birth too. Whispering among themselves, and fearful that neither would live for any length of time, the question kept being repeated, 'What should the laddie be called?'

At last, Catherine opened her eyes. She looked around the room and gave a weak but determined smile, 'His name? What should it be but Stewart in honour of the cause?'

So young Thriepland was named in honour of the dynasty his father had fought to restore. When he reached manhood, for both he and his mother gained strength quickly after the birth and he grew to be a healthy man, he too was ready and willing to fight for the Jacobite cause. His elder brother David paid the ultimate price for such loyalty, dying at the battle of Prestonpans, and Stuart, who had qualified as a doctor, attended Prince Charlie for a while after Culloden and followed him to France stayed in Rouen for a while. Returning to Scotland after the General Indemnity of 1747, he became a successful medical practitioner, successful enough that he managed to buy back the Fingask Estate in 1783. He remained a Jacobite all his days, still avowing the cause up to his death in 1805 at the grand old age of eighty-nine, a man who had been born, lived and died a Jacobite.

The Seven Men
of Glenmoriston

When Prince Charles was on the run, with the price of thirty
thousand pounds on his head, he had help from a variety of
people. None of them were more important than those who have
come down in tradition as the Seven Men of Glenmoriston.
Patrick Grant, Hugh, Alexander and Donald Chisholm, Alexander MacDonald, Gregor McGregor and John MacDonald,
who sometimes passed himself off as a Campbell, had all been in
the Jacobite army during the '45. They had returned to their
native Glenmoriston after the disbandment at Ruthven and had
seen the betrayal and slaughter of friends and relations, the
destruction of their homes and the loss of their property at first
hand. They then made a vow to stand together against the
Redcoats till the last drop of their blood. All swore this oath on
the blade of their dirks, the most solemn oath a Highlander
could make, and began what we nowadays call a guerrilla
campaign against the Government soldiers. In addition to having been raised in the warrior traditions of the Highland clans,
they had all served for some time in the Independent Highland
Companies that had been raised in the 1730s, ostensibly to bring
peace to the Highlands. They were thus trained soldiers as well
as Highland warriors, and several of them, like Gregor Mac-
Gregor, had been serving in the British Army when the prince

200

had raised his standard. On hearing of this they had immediately deserted.

From the point of view of the Government they were deserters and there would have been no point in them surrendering to be shot, but, rather than any fear for their own lives, what made them become raiders was the carnage that spread through the Highlands after Culloden. They formed a tight-knit and highly efficient fighting band for their small numbers were offset by their knowledge of the ground and their extensive knowledge of the enemy's tactics. Like all successful guerrillas, they also had the support of the local population, though due to the raids of Government troops there was often little they could do to help the Seven Men of Glenmoriston. However, they could still hunt for deer, and they were adept at picking up provisions belonging to the army they had once been part of. Throughout all of this their greatest hatred was reserved for those of their own kind who acted for the Government. The Government had great need of Gaelic-speaking natives because there were whole straths and glens where no one understood a word of English, or even Scots. Those who answered this need were traitors and deserved death, the Seven Men of Glenmoriston thought.

They hid out in *Uamh Ruaraidh na Silg*, the Cave of Roderick the Hunter, in one of the wild corries round the headwaters of the River Doe. This wilderness country to the north of Glenmoriston was ideal for their purposes. With nothing other than animal tracks through the heather, woods and scrub, it would be folly for anything short of a small army to pursue them, particularly as the red coats of the soldiers would make easy targets for the shooting skills of the Seven Men of Glenmoriston.

Now, they might have been living in a wild part of the country but they all knew how to live off the land, and now and again they even had a treat or two. One time, they were watching from the hills overlooking Loch Cluanie when they saw a party of seven Redcoats, led by a man they knew as Alexander MacPherson from Skye, with a pair of heavily laden horses. This small detachment was on its way from Glen Elg to Fort Augustus with officers' provisions. They were easy pickings for the Glenmoriston men. They made their way to a suitable spot and waited behind some boulders as the column approached. Once they were in range three of them fired off a volley and two of the Redcoats fell dead. The other four then fired and the surviving soldiers and MacPherson took off at a run towards the east, not even looking over their shoulders.

Down the hillside they came to see what they had collected. Apart from some fine wheaten bread, canned meats and sweetmeats, there were four large leather hampers, which were padlocked shut. What could this be but gold?

It was a simple matter to prise the padlocks off with their dirks, and they pulled the lids off and looked in. There was no gold. The hampers were, instead, full of bottles of wine. They buried the dead soldiers, took their weapons and, carrying the food and wine, set off back to their cave, slapping the horses to send them off in the same direction as the soldiers had fled. Now, they might have been disappointed but, as Grant said in later years, 'Well, at least we lived like princes for the next few days.'

It was only a couple of weeks after this that they saw a man crossing the area known as *Feith Bob*, Robert's Bog. They all recognised him as Robert Grant, a native of Strathspey, who had come into the area working as a translator for the Army. There was no hesitation, and the man was shot and killed from a distance. Collaborators were no more than traitors to their own kind as far as the men of the cave were concerned, and, as a warning to others, they beheaded Grant and stuck the head in the cleft of a tree close by the roadside on Loch Cluanie, between Innerwick and Duncathick. The people of the area knew fine well what this grisly sight conveyed, and those who did not directly support the Seven Men in their activities would now think more than twice about speaking to the Government representatives in the area!

It was only three days after killing Robert Grant that Patrick Grant heard that a detachment of soldiers had taken his uncle Patrick's cattle and were taking them by the recently built Wade Road through Glenmoriston. Patrick saw this as a direct challenge to him and his companions, and they decided to take a hand in the matter. The troops were a combined force of regulars and Highlander militia, raised from clans loyal to the Hanoverian cause. They numbered three officers and about sixty men, accompanying about the same number of cattle, and were already well on their way. By the time the Seven Men caught up with them they were approaching the Hill of Lundie. The seven of them took a position on the side of the hill above the road and called out to the men below, 'Hand over those cattle now, or it will be the worse for you.'

Now, the soldiers heavily outnumbered the Highlanders, but their officer could not be absolutely sure that the small group he could make out on the hill above were all that there were. Perhaps there were others in the heather. So, he decided to pay things safe. He sent Donald Fraser, a Gaelic-speaking militiaman, up the hill a bit to talk to the rebels.

'The lieutenant has said that if you are prepared to give up your weapons and surrender,' he called out, 'he will make sure that you are shown the utmost mercy and royal clemency.'

This was met with hoots and jeers, and Patrick Grant pointed his cocked weapon directly at him.

'We'll just see who needs mercy when the rest of the lads catch up. They are not far behind us. Now tell that southron fool to leave the cattle and get off to wherever you are going. It will be the worse for many of you if you do not.'

As Fraser turned to go back down the hill to report to his lieutenant, Patrick spoke again. 'Wait. Just stand there and don't move.'

Keeping his gun levelled, he came up to Fraser and stuck his free hand in the militiaman's knapsack, pulling out a half pound of tobacco.

'Very nice,' he said, sniffing the plug. 'You can go now,' he went on, stuffing the tobacco into his sporran.

The troops headed on their way up the hill; their officers had no intention of giving into such a puny force. So, the seven carried out a flanking movement above them, firing in sequence so that there was a continuous series of musket balls flying over their heads. Still the troops pressed on, even after a few of their number had been wounded, and they began to return fire. The advantage of tartan against heather and scrub had always been that it served as a form of camouflage, and as the Highlanders were also sure-footed and fast none of them were injured. Things carried on like this for a short while then, suddenly, the firing from above stopped, and, as the officers watched, the seven indistinct figures up on the hill ran forwards and over a rise in the hill. Soon they were out of sight. But not for long.

As the soldiers and the cattle came up the track, they saw the road went through a narrow pass. And from the rocks on either side of the pass muskets began to flash. The soldiers were not used to this kind of warfare, and, despite their officers' best efforts, some of them turned and ran. The cattle were spooked and broke out in all directions.

The officers regrouped their men back down the road as the cattle scattered through the heather making a great noise. Another of the militiamen was sent forward to parley with the rebels. This time it was an officer, a MacDonald, who approached and called for a parley.

'What is it you are wanting?' shouted Hugh Chisholm. 'We have said all that we are wanting to say.'

'I have been sent by the commanding officer to ask if you are mad taking on this many of the king's troops?' came the reply.

'Well, if your king came here now he would get just the same,' Gregor MacGregor spoke.

'Well then,' replied MacDonald, 'I have been told to offer you clemency again, but don't believe it for a minute. If you surrender you will be bound and gagged and carried off for trial.' MacDonald had been sickened by the behaviour he had witnessed over the previous months and had a growing sympathy for the rebels.

'If the firing starts again, aim for the taller of the two officers. Kill him and the others will run. I will try and keep my men away from the Redcoats and we will fire in the air. I will go back now and tell them you intend to fight for the cattle. Good luck.'

The Glenmoriston men looked at each other as he went back to the main force. This was a turn up. So they decided to wait and see what had happened.

MacDonald returned to the other soldiers. There, he made it very clear that the rebels had no intention of either letting the detachment pass or leaving and were prepared to die to a man to try and get the cattle. Having seen some of his men run off and not being too sure of the loyalty of the militiamen, the commanding officer decided that there would be no point in attacking the men in the pass. He might succeed in killing them, but, given their position and clear intention, it would be a costly victory. If they tried to drive the cattle back they would be presenting clear targets to the well-hidden marksmen behind them. The final upshot was that the officer made the best of a bad job and decided to hand the cattle over.

He ordered MacDonald to get his militiamen to gather up the cattle to hand over to their adversaries. In the course of this being done, two of the Glenmoriston nipped out from their positions and captured two of the militiamen. And it might not be pushing things to think that the militiamen put up no great struggle.

The Seven Men then called for another parley and demanded that they be given some of the detachment's provisions in exchange for their hostages. This further enraged the already furious commanding officer, but he was forced to agree, and a short while later the entire detachment of troops headed back the way they had come, leaving the Seven Men of Glenmoriston with the entire herd of cattle and the bonus of a horse laden with provisions! Through their knowledge and experience of the lie of the land and their sheer bloody-mindedness, the seven of them had got the better of sixty of their enemy.

Not long after this, on 28 July, the weather had turned bad. Alexander Chisholm and the two MacDonalds were sitting by the fire in their cave with the rain pouring down, their companions having gone off foraging, when they heard a shout. Grabbing their weapons, they peered out into the rain to see a distant cousin of John MacDonald's from Glengarry. He was welcomed in out of the rain and offered some mutton and whisky.

'Thanks, lads,' he said, 'but not at this moment. I have been out on the hill with Glenaladale and his brother, John MacDonald of Borrodale, and another young gentleman for the past three days. We are all sore in need of food and shelter, particularly the young gentleman. Can I bring them in?'

'Of course you can,' said Chisholm, 'we have plenty of food, though I am sorry to say we don't have any spare clothes. The fire is good and warm and we are safe here.'

So, the man from Glengarry went back up onto the hilltops above Glen Dho, where his party had spent a miserable night in a damp cave that was little more than an overhanging of the cliff, and a short while later returned with his companions.

As they came into the cave, John MacDonald leapt to his feet, his face turning bright red. His companions reached for their arms and then looked at who had come into their cave. They, too, had thought the unnamed visitor might have been young Clanranald, the son of the chief of the local MacDonalds; they had not expected it to be Charles Edward Stewart.

'Your Highness,' stuttered John, 'it is sorry I am to see you in this state, and I hope to see you in better soon. I last saw you at the head of the troops on Glasgow Green, and, and,' his voice caught with emotion for a second, then he went on, 'and I thought, then, that I would follow you wherever you might lead, but I never thought to see you here. Come in, my prince. Come in, sit by the fire and eat, we have plenty food.'

All three were on their feet as the prince nodded and smiled as Glenaladale translated John's words. Nodding again, he sat down, clearly exhausted, and the three Glenmoriston men set about giving their guests food and drink. Once they had eaten and had a drink of whisky, it was explained that the party were heading to the west, where they had hopes that a French ship was waiting for them off Poolewe. As they hadn't eaten for forty-eight hours and had had little sleep, they were all exhausted, particularly the prince, who, though he could keep up a good pace in the daylight hours, had struggled over the rough ground after dark when they had been forced to do much of their travelling over the previous weeks. So, they all lay down on the simple beds of heather and slept peacefully for the first time in quite a while.

In the morning, Glenaladale asked if it would be possible for the three of them to take them onward, as their guide was not sure of the country to the west. John MacDonald replied, 'We hear what you are saying, but we can do nothing till we have consulted with our companions. We have sworn an oath to stick together till death and we cannot desert them, not even for the prince himself. You understand?' This last was said with a hard look, and Glenaladale realised that they had sworn on their dirks. Once Charles had been informed of the situation he realised he had to accept it, and he asked if they would swear loyalty to him. This the three of them were happy to do, and, though to today's ears the words are somewhat clumsy and archaic, there can be no doubt of the sincerity with which this oath was taken. They swore 'that our backs shall be to God and our faces to the Devil, and that all the curses the Scriptures did pronounce may come upon us and all our posterity if we do not stand firm with the prince in the greatest dangers, and if we do discover to any person – man, woman or child – that the prince is in our keeping, till once his person shall be out of danger'. In fact, nothing was said about the prince's sojourn in the hills above Glenmoriston for over a year after he had successfully left the country.

Impressed by these brave and loyal supporters, Prince Charlie proposed that he and Glenaladale should themselves swear 'that if danger should come upon them they should stand by one another till the last drop of blood'.

They were told with a smile that there was no need of any reciprocal oaths.

The prince told Glenaladale to tell them that if he was successful in coming into his own inheritance he would never forget their service. At that, Chisholm said he had heard that Charles II had said something of the sort before he regained his throne and that those he had promised were still waiting. Glenaladale and his brother were a bit put out at this statement, but, when the prince insisted they tell him what had been said, he replied, nodding, 'I am heartily sorry for that, and I hope I myself will not follow the same measures and you can depend on my word as a prince.'

A day passed while they waited for the others to return. When, at last, they came, they were leading an ox through the heather and carrying most of a fine stag on their shoulders. It didn't take long for them to be put in the picture. They were all happy to take the same oath as their companions, and the ox was slaughtered. Apologies for the lack of salt and bread were made, but the prince said he was more than happy to share whatever was available. Then, however, the discussion turned to what was to be done next. The prince was most insistent that there was no time to be wasted: he wanted to head west as soon as possible. The four who had been out foraging, however, had seen several patrols and were equally insistent that there was no way anyone could leave the safety of the cave high in the hills for a few days at least. When the prince tried to command them to his will he was told in no uncertain fashion that he would be tied up to prevent him going, for there was no doubt that he would come to harm and they would not – could not – allow that. There was a deal of tension in the air when Charles Edward Stewart, always known as a man of considerable charm, calmed everyone down by saying these words. 'I find kings and princes must be ruled by their Privy Council, but I believe there is not in the world a more absolute Privy Council than what I have at present. I accept your advice gentlemen.'

So, this stay in the hills continued for a few more days, some of them spent in another cave in a nearby corrie, because, as the Glenmoriston men told their prince, there was no point in not being as careful as possible in the circumstances. While they were still at the head of Corrie Dho, Hugh Chisholm went down to get some bread, salt and other food for their guests from John Chisholm, whose farm at Fassanacoil had escaped the destruction that had been carried out in so much of the area. Here, he was told that one Lieutenant Campbell was in the area, only a few miles away, with a large herd of cattle that was being driven south. This, of course, had neither been lifted, nor stolen, but appropriated in a totally legal fashion by men in Redcoats, who had the law on their side, as well as guns. Returning with the news, he and John MacDonald then went off to take a look. They came back a few hours later saying the countryside appeared to be clear of troops. It was now safe to move on.

They headed off over the hills to Strathglass, and a couple of days later Glenaladale and Borrodale went on ahead to find out if there was any news of the ship. They returned to where the rest of the company were resting in some shieling huts with the news that two gentlemen had landed from a French ship and headed towards Cameron country round Loch Eil looking for the prince. So now they had to retrace their steps, with the Seven Men of Glenmoriston spread out around the others as scouts. Messages were sent to Cameron of Clunes to see if a meeting could be arranged. By now they were all sleeping rough and their food was low. Once again, though, the Glenmoriston men came through when Patrick Grant brought down a deer at a distance of nearly half a mile.

Then, on 20 August, Prince Charles at last met with the men who had come to take him to the waiting ship. Dugald MacCullonoy, as he had insisted on being called while with the Glenmoriston men, was effusive in his thanks and insisted that Patrick Grant come with him till he could find some funds to recompense these loyal men for their troubles. He then took a solemn farewell of them, and they headed back to their cave. It was a while till the prince managed to get away, and it was not until a few days later that Patrick Grant returned to the Cave of Roderick the Hunter, with the truly princely sum of three guineas a man! This was all the money that the prince could find spare, and it was fair way short of the thirty thousand pounds that the Government had put on the head of Prince Charles Edward Stewart! The Seven Men of Glenmoriston, though, thought that they had the best of the bargain.

They returned to their guerrilla ways and, though both Alexander MacDonald and Alexander Chisholm were dead within five years, the others lived on. Most of them had to leave the area as the destruction of houses and crops and the removal of cattle had destroyed the simple self-sufficient lifestyle that had sustained the local population for centuries. Many years later, Hugh Chisholm found himself living in Edinburgh, where he could always guarantee a meal and a drink by telling of the time he was on the run with Bonnie Prince Charlie. No matter who was in the company, carpenter or lawyer, minister or cobbler, he would only shake hands with his left hand. He was proud to tell all who would listen, 'No man has shaken my right hand since it was shaken by Prince Charles Edward Stewart when he bade me farewell at Achnasoul.'

The silver buttons

⇒◆⇐

It was 1746, and Willie Mearns was twelve years old. He lived with his mother and little two sisters at Brocklas in Glen Clova, a two-roomed stone-built house overlooking a steep descent to the River South Esk. The year before, he had stood at the Milton of Clova at the head of the glen and watched his father march off with the 800 men raised by David Ogilvy to join the Jacobite army. A few months later the dreadful news of his father's death at Prestonpans had arrived, and Willie was now the man of the house, with responsibility for his mother and two wee sisters. Already in his early teens, he was a strongly built lad, showing the signs of the big powerful man he was to grow into. As he tended the small flock of sheep the family had on the slopes of the Aud, he often found himself in tears remembering his father's last words to him.

'Mind, now, Willie, look after your mum and the girls till I come back. It will be a grand day then, with a new king and better times for all of us.'

Much of the time he felt at a loss and had no one he thought he could speak to, and when Ogilvy's regiment came back to same spot in the glen to disband in 1746 he watched from a distance, angry that his father seemed to have died in vain. He had been caught up in the excitement of the army being raised for the young prince, but now he was just angry and confused. However, he knew that his father had been happy to go out to join the prince's army, and his real hatred was reserved for the Redcoats, the Government soldiers who had come into the glen a week or so after the regiment had disbanded. They had looted and pillaged most of the glen. Luckily, from Brocklas, on the other side of the river from the road up the glen, the Mearns family had seen what was happening and had managed to drive their sheep and two cows up out of reach of the marauding troops before they arrived. Still, they had lost precious goods when the soldiers stormed through their home.

Willie and his sisters could only watch from the hills above as the soldiers ransacked the house. When a soldier knocked his mother to the ground he began to run down the hill, shouting to his sisters to mind the beasts, but by the time he got there his mother was sitting alone at the front door telling him, 'Never mind, Willie, I am all right.' All that day smoke rose from houses up and down the glen as the troops set fire to haystacks, barns and houses. The next day Willie watched the troops march back out of the glen, some pushing carts laden with what they had looted. They were followed by horse-drawn carts piled high with booty, much of which was of little use to them and would soon be discarded. Willie's heart raced and his head pounded with the anger he felt, but what could a twelve-year-old laddie do against a hundred professional soldiers? 'Soldiers,' he spat, 'they are nothing but bandits and thieves.'

Within a few days, though, Willie found there was something he could do. He was out on the Hill of Craigthran, near the headwaters of the Burn of Cuillt, when he saw something moving in a gorse bush at the side of the burn. At first, he thought it was just a stoat or a weasel, but, as he looked closer, he saw that what had moved was an arm. Somebody was hiding in the gorse bushes. It could only be a rebel.

Now, Willie was bright enough to approach the man carefully.

If it was a rebel, and it had to be, the man would be armed and quite likely ready to shoot anyone he saw as a threat. Cautiously, he approached the bush and quietly said, 'Hello?'

'Who is there?' came the reply. Willie saw a movement and realised that the man had pointed a pistol in his direction. 'I am a friend,' Willie said quickly. 'My name is Willie and my father died for the Prince at Prestonpans.'

At this point the man groaned, and Willie saw the pistol drop. He moved forward and parted the bushes. There, lying on the ground, was an unshaven, well-dressed man in jacket, waistcoat and trews. On the left side of his jacket there was an ominous dark, wet patch. Willie knew right off that the man was badly wounded.

'Here,' he said, kneeling by the man and pulling out his leather water bottle from the knapsack he carried with him, 'take a drink.'

The man reached for the bottle with his right arm and took it, raising it to his lips and gulping furiously. He then gave a cough and fell back, letting the bottle fall. As he lay there, he looked directly at Willie for the first time and gave a slight smile.

'Well, Willie, will ye help me?' he asked.

'I will do whatever I can,' said the lad. 'I have some bread and cheese here in my bag. Can you eat?'

The man nodded and Willie gave him some bread and cheese, which he gobbled down furiously. It was clear he had not eaten in some time. Once he had eaten, he fell back as if tired out with the effort, and his eyelids fluttered as if he would fall asleep. That was not a good idea, Willie thought, and he said to the semi-comatose stranger, 'Look, can you move? My home is less than two miles off and I can give you a hand. My mother will be able to take a look at your wound, but if you stay here . . .'

The man looked him in the eye. 'Are there any Redcoats about?'

'There's a corporal and four men, but they are at the head of the glen and they never come down this far,' the young lad replied. 'If we wait till the gloaming and are careful, we can keep out of sight of the road for most of the way. Can you manage it?'

'It seems I have no real choice,' replied the man with a grim smile.

He was obviously in great pain, and once the day had begun to fade it was a hard job for Willie to help him down the hillside. Most of the time he was virtually carrying the man. By the time they were close to Brocklas the man's face was deathly white and his breath was coming in great laboured gasps. Willie was also aware that the damp patch on his left side was spreading. As they neared the house, one of Willie's sisters saw them coming and ran indoors to fetch her mother. She came running up the hill to give Willie a hand in carrying the stranger the last couple of hundred yards to the house. By now, the last of the gloaming was on them and it would soon be dark. At the house they carried him in and laid him on the simple box bed in the main room. As they laid him down he gave a groan and passed out.

Mrs Mearns looked at her son with a look he had never seen before, but she only said, 'Fetch me hot water and get an old sheet from the kist, Willie. Girls, light a candle.'

Carefully, in the soft light of the candle, she cut the man's jacket away and undid his blood-soaked waistcoat. Under it, his fine linen shirt was totally soaked with blood, much of it congealed, but there was still some of it seeping through. She cut away the shirt to expose a hole in the man's side the size of a musket ball. Lifting him as gently as she could she pulled the shirt from his back. There was bigger hole, which was oozing blood from round a half-formed scab.

'He's lucky,' she said, 'the ball went straight through. We can probably save him.'

So she cleaned and bandaged the wound, and when she was

done she draped a blanket over the man, who had by now fallen into a deep, troubled sleep.

'Now, girls,' she said, 'nobody is to hear we have this visitor, it is to be our secret. And tomorrow and the days after I want you to keep an eye out for anyone coming to the house. If anyone does come you are to run and tell me. Do you understand?'

The two young lasses, Kirsty, nine, and Isabel, eight, both nodded. They had seen enough trouble in their short lives to know that keeping this man's presence secret was important.

'All right then, have your supper and be off to bed with the pair of you,' she said, as she lifted the clothing of the man from beside the bed. She proceeded to wash them in the big tub that sat at the front door before hanging them inside the house. All the time, she was deep in thought and said nothing to her son. He spent much of the time looking at the stranger in the bed and thinking of his father. Later, though, the pair of them talked deep into the night. Before going to sleep, Willie hid the man's clothing and his pistol in a hollow tree on the hillside above the house.

For the next few days the girls kept an eye out as the man was fed with soup. By the second day he was sitting up and managed to eat some lamb stew. It turned out he was from Edinburgh, a bookseller by trade, but his family were Episcopalians, and he had headed straight to Glenfinnan as soon as he had heard the prince was raising his standard. He had been travelling south through Glen Esk towards Dundee, where he had some friends, when he had been seen by a patrol and shot. He had tumbled down the bed of a stream and had managed to crawl nearly ten miles to where Willie found him.

For nearly a fortnight the Mearns family took care of their visitor, and when at last he got ready to leave he took a *sgian dubh* from inside his jacket and cut the twelve silver buttons off his waistcoat.

'These are for you,' he said, giving six to Mrs Mearns and the other six to Willie, 'it is little enough for what you have done for me, but they might help you live a little better in these hard times.'

Despite their protests that they were only giving him the necessary hospitality of tradition, he insisted they take the silver buttons. Taking Mrs Mearns by the hand, he smiled and said, 'If I had been found you and Willie would have been jailed at the very least, and well you know it. I am forever in your debt.'

And a hundred years later, when she told the story to her grandchildren, Granny Mearns would pull out the last three of the silver buttons to show how true the tale was.

Son of a hero

⇒·◇·⇐

After the slaughter at Culloden on 16 April, the British Army spread out through the Highlands on the rampage. No one was safe, and many people left their homes and hid out in the hills, often with little or no shelter. The red-coated troops tended to concentrate on the settlements in the glens, most of them ill at ease when in the rougher parts of the mountains. This meant that many families managed to escape their ravages, though no one has any idea of how many died through exposure and starvation up in the hills in the bitter spring of 1746. One family which headed in to the hills was that of Tirnadris, the hero of High Bridge. His first wife had died after bearing him three daughters and one son, Ranald. He had remarried and had two further daughters. His second wife, Beathag, fled into the hills with the six young children: Ranald, who was about seven at the time, and his three elder sisters and two younger half-sisters. On hearing of the activities of the Redcoats, she realised that their home would definitely be a target for reprisals. With the help of her children, she gathered together all their cattle and sheep, and, loading their few horses with as much provisions, bedding and clothes they could manage, they left Tirnadris and headed into the hills of Glenfintaig to spend the night. The next day, they headed south-east through Glen Spean to the shores of Loch Treig, keeping out of sight as much as possible. As they went, they could see plumes of smoke in many directions where houses were burning. They camped out in the woods on the shore of Loch Treig, unsure of what was to happen next. After about a week, a man came to where they were in the woods. Beathag gathered the children round her as the man approached. He was wearing Highland dress and, as he came close, she recognised him as one of the men who had accompanied her husband when he left their home.

'Good heavens, it is yourself, Angus Roy,' she said. 'I had been told you had been killed up at the battle near Inverness.'

'Ach, no, Beathag,' he replied, with a concerned look around, 'I managed to get away and come back home, though there were many that didn't. How are you coping out here in the woods? I saw your fire from my own home on the far side of the loch. Luckily we haven't been visited by these damned red-coated swine yet. Now look, why don't you all come over. You can't be comfortable out here in the woods.'

'Well, we have the beasts with us, and I think it better not to move them where they could be seen,' said Beathag in a worried tone of voice.

'Well then,' said Angus, well aware of the need to be careful, 'why don't you and young Ranald and the wee one come over for the night? The girls can tend to the beasts, and then they could come over for a bit of a rest in a day or two.'

Reluctant as she was to leave any of her charges behind, Beathag saw the sense in this. If she went to Angus's house she could try and make it down to her sister's house a couple of miles further on down Loch Treig to see how she was. So she agreed and went with Angus, taking Ranald and the littlest of her daughters, who was only about four. After a good meal, she and Ranald went off to see her sister. They got to her sister Morag's house, only to find that she had come down with smallpox. Fear of infection meant that they didn't stay long, just long enough to realise that, though she was badly ill, Morag would likely live.

On their way back to Angus's place, Ranald began to complain of a sore back. Within minutes he was having trouble walking and Beathag had to half-carry him back to Angus's. It was obvious that something was badly wrong with the lad: he was boiling hot and in considerable pain. They feared the worst. Soon it was clear that he had been infected with the smallpox and within a couple of days spent in a fever he went blind. For more than a week he was tended by his stepmother in a wee barn nearby. No one else was allowed close, in case they too became infected. On the far side of Loch Treig his sisters were still camped out looking after the beasts, undisturbed by the marauding bands of Redcoats. After ten days, however, Ranald's fever broke and he regained his eyesight. In later years Ranald said that the usual Highland treatment for all ills, *uisge beatha,* the water of life, what we now call whisky, was in very short supply and none could be found to dose him. However, he said, 'I just had to get on with things as best I could.'

By now, there were considerable numbers of people living rough, having been forced from their homes by the soldiers, and a handful of others from back near Tirnadris had joined the camp. There were many people who had nothing and were starving. All agreed with Beathag that the best way of keeping what they had – their cattle, sheep and horses – was to get away to Rannoch. This is a wild and rugged place with no real paths, dotted with lochans and pools, and it had long been used as a hideout by the wildest of the clan raiders. It was a place the Government troops were reluctant to go, as its wildness made it an easy place to set up ambushes, and those who knew it could disappear like morning mist if chased.

So, as soon as Ranald was fit enough, splitting up into two groups, they headed to Rannoch, following the old secret trails that had been used by the caterans or cattle-raiding clansmen since time immemorial. Beathag thought it better to send Ranald and his eldest sister, Isabella, with a distant cousin of her own who had turned up, while she and the others herded the stock. She was sure that her husband's heroics at High Bridge would mean the Government were seeking out his family and she worried what they might do to Ranald as Tirnadris's only son.

Several times on their road east they were within earshot of roaming groups of British soldiers, who were looting and pillaging wherever they went. Luckily, Beathag's cousin was well versed in the raiding ways himself, though there were several uncomfortable nights before they came to Rannoch. On the way, they met the son of MacDonald of Keppoch and his family. The meeting was brief as the others were heading north to a place they thought safe. Although people would help each other when possible, everyone was in the same desperate situation, and the only imperative was survival. When Ranald's party got to Rannoch they met up with Beathag and the others, and they hid out for a few days in an old stone- and turf-built bothy. There was enough rough pasture for their cattle, sheep and horses, but they had to be kept under close watch for it was all too easy for them to wander off over the moor never to be found again. They had not been there for more than a few days when Angus Roy turned up with his brother Samuel.

His first words after saying hello to them all were, 'Things have quietened down a wee bit around Loch Treig, and you could come back to my place for a while.'

So, the following morning the whole group set off back to the west, Ranald riding on the back of a wee Galloway pony. After his illness, the journey had worn him out and he was hardly capable of walking. In the woods that same evening they saw some Highlanders at a distance driving a herd of cattle up into the hills and decided it was best to stop where they were. Angus and the other men built a couple of rough wooden shelters against the rain, and they settled down, the children carefully tending the animals and all the time keeping their eyes open for any troops. For a couple of weeks they lived in the woods before returning to the shores of Loch Treig.

One day, Ranald, who still had not recovered all his strength, was driving some of the cattle onto an island in the fast-flowing river when he lost his footing and fell. He was carried away by the power of the cold water. Luckily, Samuel, Angus Roy's brother, was nearby and managed to pull him from the water, but it had been a close thing.

There was one strange thing, though, that puzzled Ranald. The regular soldiers of the British Army might have left the immediate district but just up on the other side of the river there was an encampment of Government Militia, Highlanders like themselves but in the pay of the Hanoverian Government. Even more startling was the fact that Angus Roy seemed to be supplying them with food. It was only in later years that he was to find out that, under instructions of Campbell of Achallader, a lifelong friend of his father's, the family of Tirnadris were in effect being protected from other Government troops by the presence of these men.

By now, word had come that Tirnadris had been burnt to the ground, so there was little point in trying to head back towards Loch Lochy. Beathag was still very concerned that Ranald should not be found, and one day he received incredible news. Two men dressed in the Lowland fashion arrived at the encampment on Loch Treig, and Beathag said to him, 'Well, Ranald, it is best that you go away from here, at least for the present. Your sisters and I will do well enough here with Angus Roy nearby, but you are to go with these two gentlemen to friends of ours in the south.' Just then, his uncle, Ranald Angus, Beathag's brother, and a young man who could speak English turned up. He was to go with them. Although still only a boy, Ranald had been brought up with ideas of kinship and honour that made him realise that, as the surviving male, he was, in effect, the head of his family. It was imperative that he survive if his family was to ever regain the lands and status they had once held.

So, after saying a sad goodbye to his sisters and stepmother, and thanking Angus Roy for all he had done, the young son of Tirnadris left the Highlands and headed towards Edinburgh. Here, he was kitted out in what he thought of as English clothes, finding the tight shirt and trousers and leather shoes both unfamiliar and uncomfortable. His father's status and reputation made him a lad of some importance, and he was shown round quite a few houses in Edinburgh where the flame of Jacobitism still flickered, even if it was behind closed doors. Much of this was confusing to the young lad for, even with instruction from Ranald Angus and others, he still had little command of English and was further confused by the Scots spoken by so many people in Edinburgh. He was taken briefly to Carlisle before ending up at Traquair, in the Borders, where he was sent to school and taught English. Being young and bright, and now in a more settled environment, he soon began to master the new tongue. Tirnadris had left instructions with his wife that he wanted the young lad educated and hoped that he would choose the life of a soldier. He had known how slim Prince Charles's chances were and had thought that, if anything happened to him, Ranald could become a soldier and he would perhaps in time have the chance to fight for the cause himself in later years. This was not how it worked out.

Ranald had been at Innerleithen for more than a year and was showing himself to be a good student when a stranger turned up. Yet again, it seemed, he was to move. His companion on his travels this time was a man who was passing himself off as a wandering fiddler, a good cover for keeping in touch with Jacobite sympathisers all over Lowland Scotland and northern England. The fiddler took him over the border to Warwick Hall near Carlisle. This was the home of Francis Warwick and his wife Jane, who, like Ranald and his family, were Catholics. Any concern the Warwicks might have felt about supporting the Jacobite cause had disappeared after the bloody assize at Carlisle, when so many Catholic Highlanders were hung out of hand, and they had agreed to carry on with the lad's education and ensure that he was brought up in the faith of his fathers.

Having no children of their own, they raised Ranald as if he was their own son and spared no expense on his education. In his mid teens, to finish off his education, they sent him to France, to a college in Douai, and it was here that Ranald at last made his decision as to a career. He did not want to be a soldier, but he would make his own contribution to the ongoing struggle. What better way to do that than enter for the priesthood? Like many another, Beathag would have been proud of his decision, even as she realised that the line of Tirnadris would die out. However, it was not long after this that Ranald was struck down with a fever, and, already weakened by his earlier fight with smallpox, he passed away before he had been ordained. The efforts of his family and their friends to ensure his safety, and carry on the Tirnadris line, by taking him to England had worked, but only for a few years.

A loyal lass

⟫◆⟪

On his way south towards England Prince Charlie had stopped with his army in Dunblane, where he stayed in Strathallan's Lodgings in Millrow. One of the servant lasses there, Effie, was given the task of polishing his boots. Late at night, after the prince was asleep, she came into his room to get the boots. Looking on the sleeping prince her heart was filled with emotion, and she could not bear to tear herself away. So, she sat and polished his boots by the light of a candle. In the morning, he awoke to see her still sitting there, gazing at him wide-eyed. He reached out his hand towards her, but she flushed and fell to her knees, still holding one of his boots.

'Come, lass, and take my hand,' he smiled at her.

Effie could not bring herself to speak, or even take the offered hand, and simply contented herself with kissing his boot, her face bright red and her eyes glistening.

'What is wrong, lass,' he went on, 'are you scared of me?'

'Och no, my Prince. Och no, that's not it at all. I am scared to my heart for you. You are going against the English and there are ten of them for every one of your own men. I fear for you my Prince.' She lowered her head and muffled a sob.

'You need not worry, my dear,' the prince said, 'once I have gone into England there are many there who will come forward to support my father's cause. Do not worry yourself.'

She got to her feet, put down the boot she had been holding and curtsied to the prince before scampering from the room. Charles Edward Stewart smiled to himself. This was good sign, he thought, that even the servants are supporting us. However, he had much on his mind and soon forgot all about Effie.

It was more than a year later when the Jacobites returned to Dunblane. This time, though, there was no great celebration. They were grim-faced and tired-looking and stayed one night before moving north. Behind them came the great army of the Duke of Cumberland, set on destroying what he saw as a treasonous rebellion by ingrates and savages. And, as they came, they looted and pillaged at will. As far as the duke was concerned, all of these Scots were traitors to his father and deserved whatever they got. He was already, even at the young age of twenty-four, a man of brutal simplicity and utter arrogance.

He, too, came to Dunblane and stayed overnight in the town. In the morning, two men who had been caught stealing from the army baggage train were brought before him in his lodgings. They were a rough-looking pair, both dressed in the simple hodden grey that was almost a uniform for the common people of the time. Each of them was firmly held on each side by a soldier.

'Right,' he said, pointing at one of the men, 'what is your name?'

'B-B-B-Brown, Your Highness,' stuttered the man.

'Ah, good. Brown,' said the duke, 'that is a good English name. We have many Browns in our troops.' He smiled and turned to his aide-de-camp. 'Let this man go free.'

The aide-de-camp nodded to the soldiers holding Brown and he was marched out of the room.

'Now, you,' he barked, pointing at the remaining man, 'what is your name?'

'My name is McNiven, Sire,' replied the man, bowing his head.

'McNiven, McNiven,' roared the duke. 'That is a filthy thieving Highland name. Take him out and hang him.'

McNiven's head shot up and looked at the duke, who waved his hand, and, as the man's legs collapsed under him with fear, he was dragged out by the soldiers. They dragged him to a nearby tree and, with no further ceremony, strung him up while his companion looked on, a free man. Returning to his breakfast as if nothing had happened, Cumberland calmly finished his meal. Then, he stepped outside and mounted his magnificent grey charger.

Waving to his officers to follow him, he headed off eastwards along Millrow. As he went, he passed by Strathallan's Lodging. Just as he got there a figure appeared in a window above him. It was Effie. In her hands she had a pan of boiling oil. Quickly, she leaned out of the window and tipped the pan. The searing liquid poured down, missing Cumberland by a couple of inches. It didn't miss his horse. The poor creature let out a terrified squeal and reared up, spilling his rider into the dirt. As he sprawled in the street, the officers behind him started shouting, 'After her, after her. Surround the building.'

Soldiers battered down the door of the lodgings as others ran in either direction to get round the back of the house. Boots thundered up the stairs to the room where the would-be assassin had stood. There was no one there. By the time the rest of the soldiers got round the back of the house, Effie had made her escape by ducking into the underground culvert through which the Mannie Burn ran to the Allan Water. Through this, she escaped into open countryside. Behind her the troops fanned out through the houses on either side of Strathallan's Lodging, smashing doors and windows as they went. They found nothing and proceeded to wreck the three houses. Things would have been even worse for Dunblane had not Cumberland himself ordered his men to stop. He had given his word to the local Laird, Drummond, a staunch Hanoverian, that Dunblane would not be torched and, despite the attempted assault, he stuck to his word.

As for Effie, she got clean away. Once all the troubles had settled down, she married a wealthy local farmer and lived a long and happy life, giving birth to several children, but never forgetting the effect that Prince Charlie had had on her in her youth.

It is well known locally that Prince Charlie left a special present behind him in Dunblane. A present that nine months later came into the world as a healthy baby boy, who went on to become a minister of religion in Glasgow and who never denied his parentage.

DARK DEEDS

The word of an officer

———⟫◆⟪———

Many of the Clanranald MacDonalds on the island of Eigg were in the Jacobite army in the '45, and once the rebellion had failed they returned home, minus a few of their number who had given their lives for the cause. They hid their weapons and returned to the simple life of self-sufficient farming and fishing that had been the island's way of life for centuries. As ever, there were some among them who were fervent Jacobites, some who had gone along out of clan loyalty and others who had mainly appreciated the opportunity for raiding and booty. For a lot of them all three reasons would have played some part. All, however, had returned disappointed, but they would bide their time in case the call to arms came again. In June of 1746 HMS *Terror*, commanded by one Captain Duff, anchored off the island. A party of armed marines came ashore to gather up the arms that the islanders had retained. However, like many Jacobites, they had not given up hope that the prince might come again, so they only gave up enough weapons to make it appear as though they were comply-ing with the order. As there had been demands for weapons after earlier risings, most of these weapons were old and ineffective and had been bought specially for just such an occasion, and there had even been instances of old and shoddy weaponry being imported from the Continent specifically to be handed over to the Govern-ment troops. The MacDonalds on Eigg hoped that this would be enough to make the ship go off and leave them in peace to get on with their lives. This was not to be the case for a few days later the *Terror* was joined by HMS *Furnace*.

The commander of the *Furnace* was Captain John Ferguson, a Scot, who had specifically come to Eigg looking for Dr John MacDonald of Kinlochmoidart, brother of Donald, the chief who was executed at Carlisle. Ferguson had received intelligence that the doctor was hiding out on the island, and he came ashore with a large party of sailors and marines who proceeded to thoroughly search the whole island. In the course of this search considerable numbers of the useful weapons were found and the mood amongst the Navy men turned ugly. Captain Ferguson had with him the Reverend Daniel MacQueen, the minister from Rum, who had been ordered to accompany the ship as interpreter. McQueen knew MacDonald personally and, often having been on Eigg, knew the layout of the island well. In fact, he had a pretty fair idea of where the doctor might be hiding out. He managed to sneak off from the troops combing the island, and, sure enough, he found John MacDonald where he thought he would be. This was in *Uamh Fraing*, Frances's Cave, where a notable massacre of the Eigg MacDonalds had taken place nearly two centuries earlier. Giving him what he thought was sound advice, McQueen told him that it was only a matter of time before he was found and suggested it might be best for himself and everyone on the island if he gave himself up. MacDonald, not wishing to cause the islanders any more problems than they already faced, accepted the minister's argument. He accompanied him to Kildonan and surrendered to Ferguson.

At first, he was well treated. Ferguson took him into the house that had been commandeered and sat him at a table, ordering food and drink to be brought.

'Now, Captain MacDonald,' he said, 'I would like your assistance in resolving this situation. I am well aware that there are still many arms secreted about the island, and it is my bounden duty to make certain that all the men in this island have been completely disarmed under the terms of the Disarming Acts. This must be done before my men and I leave the island. Now, I will have all the men of the island brought here, and I would like you to tell them that, if they comply and hand over all their arms, I will give them full protection for both their persons and effects and that this will save them against any future danger. You, too, will not be harmed. If they do not comply, I will have my men set fire to every house on the island and help themselves to anything they see. Do you understand?'

'I will do as you ask,' said MacDonald in a heavy voice, realising that he had little choice in the matter. But he had just been given the word of an officer and a gentleman that this would put an end to the current troubled situation. At once, half a dozen young local lads were brought in and MacDonald told them that he, personally, wanted them to go and tell all the men on the island to come to him, bringing whatever weapons and ammunition they still possessed. He told them that he had been given the word of Captain Ferguson that this would lead to the Navy sailing off from the island and leaving them all in peace.

A couple of hours later a large body of men was seen approaching. As they came near, it was obvious that many of them were carrying weapons, though amongst them were a few old people and a handful of children. Ferguson gave a command and MacDonald was bundled into the house by a group of marines as the group approached. It was noticeable that there were very few young women about. They had heard of what had happened on Canna, where the crew of the HMS *Furnace* had attacked and raped several women, and thought it best to keep out of the way – well, as much as they could on a wee island like Eigg.

The men, who had also heard of what had happened on Canna,

were not enamoured of the idea of giving up their weapons, but they were prepared to put their trust in the word of Doctor John MacDonald. They accepted that the captain had given his word to him as a gentleman that they would be unharmed and agreed, though reluctantly, and with some argument among themselves, that they would do as they were asked. As they arrived at Kildonan, the older people and children were told by McQueen to return to their homes as Captain Ferguson wanted to talk to the men alone. They went off till only the men were left. One by one, they handed over their weapons to the marines and the soldiers and then stood back in a group. Once all the weapons had been gathered in, Captain Ferguson showed his true colours.

Doctor MacDonald was dragged from the house, stripped naked in front of all there and clapped in irons. Several of the Eigg men stepped forward only to find the marines coming at them with bayonets on their gun barrels. They had handed over their own weapons and could do nothing but stand and watch as the naked fugitive was dragged to one of the ship's boats and taken off to the *Commodore*, where he was thrown into the filthy bilges below decks. Things then took another turn for the worse. Going through MacDonald's clothes Ferguson found a piece of paper. On it were all the names of all the men who had been out in the Jacobite army. It had been used for the roll call among the prince's forces and MacDonald had stupidly not got rid of it. Ferguson then read out the names one by one, and the reverend McQueen instructed them to stand in a separate place from the rest of the men of the island without telling them what the list that Ferguson was reading from was. Once the list had been read and the men were standing apart Ferguson had them put in irons and shepherded at gunpoint to the ship's boats. There were great cries of anger and distress, and several of the men tried to attack their captors but were beaten to the ground. Soon all were in the boats and they set off.

Then, as the Eigg men, thirty-eight of them, were ferried out to the anchored ship, the marines and sailors still on shore began to spread out across the island. As they went, they shot all the cattle and horses, pillaged every house of whatever valuable was in it and at least a couple of women who had not hidden away were raped in broad daylight. Under the pointed guns of the red-coated marines and the blue-dressed sailors, their men folk could only watch with their hearts breaking. As for the men on board, they were taken, with little or no food or water, to London. Once there, they were tried and sentenced in the usual perfunctory manner, and the majority were sent off to work as indentured servants, another name for slaves, in the Jamaican colonies. They learned too late just how much trust they could have in the word of a British naval captain, loyal to the House of Hanover, even if he was a Scotsman.

As for Doctor John MacDonald, he spent a long year on board the prison ship *Pamela* in the River Thames. Living conditions in the prison ships, or hulks, were notoriously foul, and many Highlanders died of disease and starvation in the filthy holds where the fresh clear air of the Highlands was like a dream. It has been said that many died not of disease but of broken hearts. Whether or not that is true, Doctor John MacDonald survived for over a year in that hell-hole and, despite the Government's best efforts at compiling evidence against him, was at last set free in 1747 without being charged with any crime. Many of the Eigg men were not so lucky. To save themselves the bother and expense of trying the hundreds of Jacobite prisoners in the hulks the Government selected one in twenty by lot. These were tried, found guilty and hanged. The others were pardoned for their crimes but only on the condition that they would indenture themselves to Richard Gildart of Liverpool, Merchant, or Samuel Smith of London, Merchant, 'by which Indenture they shall bind and put themselves An Apprentice and Servant to the said Richard Gildart and Samuel Smith . . . to serve them or their Assigns in our Colonies in America'. So the majority of the Eigg men who had trusted the word of Captain Fergusson ended their days as little more than slaves in the plantations of the West Indies. After his release John MacDonald went home and in time his family regained their lands.

The tragic tale of Lady Grange

⥤•◆•⥢

Rachel Cheisley was the daughter of John Cheisley of Dalry and made what, at the time, was thought to be good marriage when she married the Honourable James Erskine of Grange, younger brother of Bobbing John, the Earl of Mar. James was admitted to the Scottish Bar in July 1705, and within a year he was raised to the Bench – no doubt through the influence of his brother, who was, at that time, Secretary of State for Scotland. In 1707 he was made a Lord of Justiciary, and in 1710 he was appointed Lord Justice-Clerk. Both he and his brother were doing very well under Queen Anne, and when the new king, George I, was handed the thrones of England and Scotland they had hopes of their good fortune continuing. However, politics is a fickle business, and when Mar found himself out of favour with the new king he rapidly turned his coat and became a Jacobite. After the debacle of the 1715 Rising he fled in disgrace to the Continent, but his younger brother, who took no part in the affair, stayed on in Scotland.

Now, Rachel was a strong supporter of the Hanoverian Government. Although she had been something of a beauty in her youth, she had a liking for the bottle, and there were those who said she proved the rumours of madness in her family. The relationship between man and wife deteriorated over time, and by 1730 they were effectively separated, if still living at adjoining addresses in Edinburgh. By now, she had developed the habit of spying on her husband, who she was convinced had long been unfaithful to her.

In 1731 she became aware that a considerable number of Jacobite-leaning men were visiting her husband, and she realised that, like his brother, James Erskine was playing the Jacobite card. Choosing her time, she managed to lay her hands on some incriminating documents concerning the planned landing of French troops. She went further and hid behind a sofa one evening when visitors came to call to ascertain just when and where this event was going to take place. Then she made a major mistake. She confronted her husband and said that if he did not renounce his Jacobite plotting at once she would head for London and denounce him to the authorities there. She was actually all set for her journey to the English capital when, on 22 January, she was grabbed, bound and gagged by a number of Highlanders who had somehow gained access to her home. She was then placed in a sedan chair and taken outside the City of Edinburgh. Here, she was put on the back of a horse ridden by a guard, who rode off through Linlithgow. Arriving at a house near Torwood, she was kept imprisoned for a few weeks. Amongst the conspirators who arranged her kidnapping were MacDonald of Morar, the Laird of MacLeod's brother, and a representative of someone who seemed to have a hand in every plot, Simon Lovat. The latter had supplied the men for the actual kidnapping. After a few weeks, the poor woman was taken further north, through Stirling, Callander and the Pass of Leny. Then, she was carried on through Glencoe to Glenfinnan.

Here, a boat arrived for her, and she was taken down Loch Shiel in a dreadful storm that forced the boatmen to come to land. However, after a rough night in the open, she was again conveyed from the boat to Acharacle and half carried over the hills to Dorlin and Castle Tioram, which had been partially restored since being set alight by the chief of Clan Ranald when he set off for the Rising of 1715. Here the lady was locked up in a tower room. One evening she heard a sound, muffled, but clearly human. She fell into a fitful sleep and was awakened by the same insistent noise. She went to the window just in time to catch a glimpse of a human figure on the nearby battlements, before it disappeared round a corner. Convinced she had seen a ghost, she ran back to her bed and hid her head under the covers, eventually managing to fall into a deep sleep. In the morning, when she awoke, she found a piece of paper on the table in the room. It read, 'Lady, if you desire escape from this place and can face danger in the accomplishment, knock on the panel behind your door at midnight and you will be heard.'

In her confusion, she was unsure if this was genuine offer of help or merely a trick on the part of her captors. She examined the wood panelling behind the door but could make out nothing unusual there. Just as night was falling she heard a noise outside and ran to the window only to see an indistinct figure walking along the battlements. It appeared to be the same one she had seen the previous night. At the appointed hour of midnight she gave a sharp rap on the panel behind the door. Nothing happened, so she rapped again. Again, nothing happened, and by now the blood was pounding in her ears with the tension. A third time she chapped on the wood, much harder than the previous times. At once the entire panel slid back revealing a narrow passage lit by a small lantern resting on the floor. Quickly, she stepped into the passage, and, as she did so, the panel slid quietly shut beside her. By now she was in a state of near terror. Unsure of what was happening to her, but steeling herself, she began to walk along the passage, holding the lantern to see her way. Soon she came to a narrow set of twisting stairs. Gingerly, she felt her way down the stairs, not knowing what to expect and fearing that something horrible was about to happen at any moment.

At last she came to the end of the stairs. Holding the lantern high she saw she was in large room, maybe even the main hall of the house, and there before her was a table. On the table lay a *sgian dubh*, glinting in the flickering light, and under it was a handkerchief. The handkerchief was stained with a dark, livid colour that she realised was blood! This just made her even more nervous; she turned away from the table and seeing a door a few paces away made straight for it. In an instant she had opened the door and gone into the room beyond. Holding the lantern high she saw she was in a rough-hewn chamber in the living rock, and, fearing the worst, she gave a small cry and dropped the lantern. It went out. Reaching out in the dark towards where she thought the door handle to be, she clasped a hanging chain that began to drop with a rattling sound that totally unnerved her. She fainted dead away.

She awoke in daylight to find herself on the floor of the room with the young woman who had been bringing her meals standing over her. Beside her was a man armed with sword and pistols. If there had been an attempt to rescue her it had clearly gone wrong, and she feared the *sgian dubh* and the blood-stained handkerchief she had seen the night before were evidence of some dark deed. Within minutes she was back in her prison at the top of the tower. Within a couple of days she was moved again, this time to a crude hut on the Isle of Skye.

Back in the capital in this period things took an ominous turn. Lord Grange put out word that his wife had been taken ill and had died. He and his fellow conspirators had then arranged a large and well-attended funeral in which a coffin filled with stones was the focus of attention. Despite this, however, rumours continued to circulate that Lady Grange was in fact alive and being kept prisoner somewhere in the Hebrides. The plotters met again and decided that Skye was too close to the mainland to keep her hidden away safely. Again, the poor woman was moved, this time for a while to the Isle of Uist. Here, she was imprisoned on the tiny island of Heiskeir, about ten miles off the west coast of North Uist.

Here, another rescue attempt took place. It involved the figure she had seen at Castle Tioram. This was an Irish sea captain, who regularly sailed the west coast of Scotland. Suspected by the Jacobites of spying on them, he had been made a prisoner in Castle Tioram and had managed to bribe a guard to let him escape, by which time he had become aware of the other prisoner in the castle. If Lady Grange had waited longer in the hall at Castle Tioram she could have escaped with him! Now he turned up at Heiskeir in unfortunate circumstances. With his Hebridean contacts, he had managed to locate where Lady Grange was being held, and he had come in a small ship with the idea of rescuing her. The plan came to nothing as he had been shipwrecked on Heiskeir itself in a vicious storm that took place just weeks after she herself had been landed on the island. The captain and his cabin boy were the only survivors of the shipwreck, and, though he tried, he could not get her off the island. He did, however, manage to get a few minutes alone with the unfortunate woman, and he promised to do his best to effect a rescue.

Word was sent to MacLeod of Dunvegan that someone had turned up on Heiskeir and appeared to know who Lady Grange was. It therefore seemed that the stranger's arrival was most likely part of an attempt at rescue. It was clear that the prisoner would have to be moved yet again.

At this point, someone came up with what appeared the ideal plan. They would ship her off to St Kilda. This remote island, forty miles out into the Atlantic off the west coast of North Uist, was the most isolated community in the whole of Britain, and the inhabitants were all monoglot Gaelic speakers. None of them spoke a word of either Scots or English. To Grange and his comrades this appeared to be the ideal place to keep Lady Grange incommunicado! She would be totally isolated with no way of even attempting to ask for help from the local people. So, she was shipped out in a small boat over rough seas to the far-off island. Here was a woman used to the intellectual cut-and-thrust of the country's capital, a woman of sophisticated tastes and interests, isolated amongst the simplest – in fact, most primitive – community in the land, where not a single soul would be able to understand what she said.

On St Kilda, she spent several miserable years, unable to communicate with more than sign language to the islanders. At last, she was moved again, this time to Waternish in Skye where life was little easier. The food was not as monotonous as it had been on St Kilda, where the people lived off a very plain diet that involved a lot of seabirds. And she had better and warmer clothes. Also, there were a few people who could speak a few words to her. Despite the privations of the previous few years, she was a strong woman and her spirit was unbroken. Having been taught to spin wool – all hands were needed in outlying communities that lived on the edge of survival – she realised that the wool she was spinning was being sent off to the market at Inverness. Somehow, she managed to get her hands on some paper and enclosed a letter in one of the hanks of wool that went off to the mainland. She had managed to get some paper, but, despite all her efforts, she could not lay her hands on any ink and was forced to desperate measures. Instead of ink, her pathetic letter was written in her own blood. In it she described where she thought she was and pleaded for help. She slipped it into a skein of wool and waited till it was picked up to be sent to the mainland. All she could do after that was pray.

The letter was addressed to one of her friends, and eventually it arrived at the address. Her friend then approached the Government with this sorry tale and a request to send a ship to look for her. Despite this clear evidence of kidnapping and Lady Grange's piteous condition, the influence of Grange, MacLeod and Mac-Donald of Sleat was such that the expedition kept being put off for one spurious reason or another. Despairing of the Government ever getting its act together, her friends decided that they would take matters into their own hands. They chartered and kitted out a small ship, and it set out for Skye. Meanwhile, at Waternish, the poor woman had no idea if her letter had even managed to get through. She must have suspected that it had the day that some of MacLeod's men came for her at Waternish and carried her off to a cave near Idrigill Point at the mouth of Loch Bracadale, fifteen miles to the south. This was long known locally as Lady Grange's Cave. She spent some time here before being moved west yet again back to North Uist.

This time, she was taken in a small boat with a rope round her neck to which was tied to a great stone. The boatmen had clear instructions. If any ship appeared and approached them they were to throw her overboard to sink to the seabed and drown. Luckily for them all, nothing happened to disturb them on the voyage. For a further couple of years Lady Grange lived her sad existence on the Uists before being finally returned to Waternish. Here, some-time not long before the Jacobite rebellion of 1745, she died. It is said that MacLeod of Dunvegan, struck by an extremely belated fit of conscience, laid on a great funeral on Skye. However, there were those among the locals that insisted that the coffin buried at Duirinish kirkyard on the mainland was filled with stones and turf and that she had, in fact, been secretly buried at Trumpan kirkyard many miles away, on the Waternish peninsula of Skye.

Rachel, Lady Grange, may have been a difficult woman but her story is essentially a tragic one, and it had a postscript that is more than a little ironic. MacDonald of Sleat and MacLeod of Dunvegan were the main movers in keeping Lady Grange prisoner for so many years. It is one of the more striking aspects of the '45 that two such active Jacobite plotters ended up on the Government side. There are those who tell that this was simply because certain Hanoverian ministers in Scotland knew what was going on all along, were perfectly aware of their complicity in this shameful deed and effectively blackmailed them into deserting the cause they supposedly supported. Whatever the truth, the presence of the Highland warriors that these two supposed gentlemen would have brought to the army of Prince Charles Edward Stewart could have made a difference to the campaign, if not its long-term outcome. But, then again, when it comes to history, who can tell?

Sergeant Davis

⟹⬥⟸

For many years after Culloden the Highlands of Scotland were under military occupation. Some of the Jacobite rebels had taken to the hills and were following the traditions of the School of the Moon. This was the name given among the Highland clans to the training for cattle-raiding, a traditional part of clan life since time immemorial. Now, though the caterans were not raiding other clans, they were lifting cattle from the Lowlands, and they were ever ready to fight the Redcoats if discovered. In the years after Culloden there were eight soldiers quartered at Dubrach near Inverey, five miles west of Braemar on the River Dee, who were under the command of Sergeant Arthur Davis, and there was another garrison eight miles away at the Spittal of Glenshee. Both parties, under the overall command of the officer in charge at Braemar Castle, regularly scoured the area. They would meet up, perhaps a couple of times a week, halfway between their locations, in the Cairnwell Pass, the only easy route through the mountains in the area. The Cairnwell had been the site of battles in the past between cattle-raiders and locals, and now it was becoming a major route for cattle-droving. At other times, the soldiers would run into the mounted patrols based at Braemar and Corgarff Castle to the north, which combed the high passes searching for the Jacobite caterans like the notorious Sergeant Mor, who regularly criss-crossed the area round the Cairnwell and Braemar.

Most of the locals fiercely resented the occupying troops and gave secret support to the men in the hills, but it seems that Sergeant Davis was basically an honourable and decent man. He and his wife, who ran the troops' billet in Inverey, were, if not exactly popular with the natives, at least tolerated. Davis, a fit and powerful man, was fond of hunting, and, within a few months of taking over the command, he had developed the habit of going off on his own into the hills with his gun to see what he could get for the pot. This was a blatant breach of regulations as there was no guarantee he would not run into rebels, or even become the target for Jacobite sympathisers within the local community, but this bothered him not at all. He trusted that the locals were not the sort to shoot a man in the back, and he had enough confidence in his own fighting abilities to reckon that, unless he ran into a large group of caterans, he would be able to hold his own.

Now, he might have been a man who was fond of outdoor pursuits but he also liked to dress well by the standards of the day. There was no need for him to wear a uniform for his day-to-day duties, and he was generally dressed in a blue coat with a silk vest, expensive breeches and a pair of gold-buckled shoes. He also carried a green silk purse, which, it was well known, contained a fair amount of money, for Sergeant Davies was man of some means. He was known to carry at least fifteen guineas in gold as well as a fair amount of silver coin for running expenses. In addition, he wore two gold rings, one of which had the inscription 'When this you see, Remember me' and the letters D H. This ring had belonged to his wife's previous husband, the paymaster of the regiment, who had passed away a few years earlier. The other ring was of a curious shape and had a heart-shaped lump of gold on it. This was a significant fact in the later story. As well as this, the bold sergeant wore silver buckles at his knees, a silver fob watch and a full two dozen silver buttons on his waistcoat, and he carried in his pocket an unusual penknife. There was also silver lacing in

244

his hat and a silver button with his initials on it on the crown. He was, in short, a bit of a dandy and must surely have presented an attractive target to robbers.

On 28 September 1749, a Thursday, he said goodbye to his wife at the house of Michael Farquharson, where they were billeted, and headed off alone towards the Cairnwell to meet the patrol from the Spittal, leaving his men to follow on behind him. He was hoping to do a bit of shooting on his way. By now, he had been going off on his own for several months and was confident he was in no danger. A while later, four of the other soldiers headed off after him. On his way that fateful morning Davis ran across John Growar in Glenclunie. Growar later testified that the sergeant had reprimanded him for wearing a tartan waistcoat. Wearing tartan, like carrying weapons without specific authorisation, was contrary to the recently passed Disarming Act and carried severe penalties, but in this case Davis let him off. Some time later his men met the patrol from Spittal and saw the sergeant waving to them from up on the hill. Shortly after, they heard a shot from the same direction, but they headed off assuming he was hunting as usual. This had happened on many an occasion before. Not long after the meeting, on their way back to their base, the soldiers from the Spittal actually ran into the sergeant by the Water of Benow and he said he was off after a deer.

The corporal in charge of the details said, 'Don't you think you are taking too much of a chance on your own out here?'

Sergeant Davis laughed off his concerns saying, 'I have done it many times before now. I am all right as long as I have my guns and plenty ammunition.' Apart from his gun, he also had a pistol in his belt.

The corporal looked at the gun the sergeant was holding in the crook of his arm and said, 'That is not a standard issue weapon is it?'

'No,' replied the sergeant, 'it is my own weapon and a damned fine one too. With a bit of luck it should help me get some nice venison today. Now, take your men back to the Spittal and we shall meet again in a few days.' Saying this the sergeant turned and headed back into the hills, and the detail marched back to the Spittal of Glenshee. They never saw Davis again. That night, when the sergeant failed to return, the worst was suspected, and two soldiers were sent to the Spittal to see if, by some chance, he had ended up staying there and, if not, to tell them he was missing. Word was also sent to Braemar and Corgarff, and when he had not returned the following day search parties were organised and a host of red-coated soldiers were to be seen combing the hills.

Four days later no trace had been found. His wife was sure that he had been robbed and murdered, but there were those in the community who said he had simply run into some of the 'men in the heather' who made short work of their enemy, adding under their breath that it had served him right.

No body was found, and a replacement sergeant was sent to Inverey with strict orders that neither he nor any of his men should ever leave their billet on their own, for any reason.

Nothing more was heard of the sergeant till June the following year. One day that month, Donald, the son of Michael Farquharson, with whom the Davies had been lodging, received a strange message. It had come from Alexander MacPherson, who was up at the sheilings above Glenclunie. Alexander wanted Donald to come up to the sheilings to discuss something with him. It all seemed very mysterious. The sheilings were the simple huts built alongside the high meadows where the livestock were taken to graze during the summer months to take advantage of the lush grass. Normally, it was young lads and lassies who tended to the livestock at the sheilings, but in such troubled times many parents were reluctant to send their children into the hills and many men went themselves. A day or so later Donald headed off to see what MacPherson wanted.

He got there to hear a story he had a great deal of trouble believing! Once he had got to the sheiling and sat down to eat, MacPherson told him that he had had a visitation from the ghost of Sergeant Davis.

'What,' spluttered Farquharson, dropping the spoon he had been eating with and spilling soup over himself.

'Aye, that's right,' said Alexander in a gloomy voice, 'the ghost of the sergeant came in to the sheiling the other night and told me, "You must go and bury my bones."'

'Och, come on now, Donald,' said Farquharson, wiping the soup off his clothes, 'you really cannot be asking me to believe that.'

'Och, yes, but I can,' said Donald, looking him straight in the eye. 'I went to where the ghost said and there the bones were, lying scattered in the heather. I will take you there once you have had your soup.'

He was so clearly telling the truth as he saw it that Farquharson nodded his agreement, finished his soup and the two of them set off into the hills, carrying the shovels Donald insisted they take

MacPherson led him to the Hill of Christie, between Glenchristie and Glenclunie, a few miles from Dubrach, and about half a mile from the road regularly taken by the patrols from Spittal and Dubrach. There, on a patch of bare earth, below a heather-covered bank, were the scattered remains of a human skeleton. Some of the hair was still attached to the skull. It was light brown and tied back with a black silk ribbon, just as Sergeant Davis's had been. There were also a few scraps of faded blue cloth and a pair of stout brogues, minus the buckles, on the feet of the skeleton. There was no doubt as to who this was.

'When did the ghost come to you?' asked Farquharson.

'About a week back,' MacPherson replied.

'Did the apparition say anything about wanting a Christian burial?' Donald then asked.

'No. It did not do that,' came the reply.

'Right, then we'll just bury him here and let no one know of this. I am sure the Redcoats would see in this a rebel murder and God knows what they would do to all of us then,' said Donald in a decisive voice, and the pair of them set to work digging into the peaty soil. With both of them digging, it didn't take long for them to have a hole big and deep enough to put the bones in. This they did carefully, if a bit reluctantly, and then filled in the soil and piled heather over the freshly dug earth. From even a few feet away there was now no sign of anything. This was all done in silence, and, once they were finished, they headed back, again without a word. At the sheilings they shook hands without speaking, and Donald Farquharson headed to his home in Dubrach, sure that nothing further would come out about this event.

What he didn't know was that MacPherson had already told another local man, John Growar, that he had found the body. They had met on the hill just after Donald had found it, and, in something of a state of shock, he had pointed out the place to Growar. The latter had then gone on to tell John Shaw of Daldownie, a man of influence in the area. He said the same as Farquharson, that the army would likely carry out repercussions if they found the body, so it was best left well alone. Despite the supposed secrecy, word was soon out, and soon Growar's brother found the sergeant's gun and a local lassie called Isabel found the remains of the sergeant's silver-laced hat while looking for some ponies that had run off to the hills. It still had its silver button intact. When she took the hat back to her family they too wanted things kept quiet and told her to dispose of it. She did so by burying it nearby, but a little while later a bunch of children playing by the Inverey Burn found it and took it into the village in all innocence.

It was only a matter of time before the hat then came into the possession of James Small, who was the Government-appointed factor on the forfeited Strowan estate, and he recognised it at once by the silver button. He had no hesitation in taking it to Braemar Castle, where he handed it over to the barrack-master, John Cook. The matter was put into the hands of Ensign Small and he began asking questions.

Word of the finding of the body was soon common knowledge, and rumours began to spread that the sergeant had been murdered. It was whispered that the deed had been done by Duncan Terig Clerk and Alexander Bain MacDonald, neither of whom were considered particularly honest men by their neighbours. MacDonald, as a forester at Allanquioch, was one of the few natives allowed to carry a gun.

However, it was four years till the case came to court, Ensign Small being the driving force in having Clerk and MacDonald prosecuted. The trial began at the High Court in Edinburgh on 10 June 1754 before several judges whose anti-Jacobite feelings had been made clear in the trial of James of the Glens the year before. The jury were picked from amongst Edinburgh tradesmen. Both Clerk and MacDonald admitted having seen the sergeant that morning, but stated that it was before ten o'clock in the morning and that the sergeant was alive when they last saw him. Effectively, they were witnesses for each other. Various witnesses were produced including one, Angus Cameron, who claimed to have seen Clerk and another man murder Davis. He said he had been one of the 'men in the heather', a rebel hiding out, when he saw the deed done. The fact that his companions 'in the heather' had all been hanged, while he had survived to be a crown witness, went some way to undermining his testimony. It seemed likely he had turned King's Evidence to save his own life. The Crown's case was further weakened by the non-appearance of a couple of witnesses, both of whom were subsequently heavily fined.

The clincher, though, was probably Isobel McHardie, who had been in the sheiling at the same time as MacPherson and claimed also to have seen Sergeant Davis's ghost, if only briefly. Unlike MacPherson, she didn't claim that Davis spoke to him in Gaelic, a detail that the jury noted hardly fitted with the fact that when alive Davis couldn't speak a word of the language. The sober industrious Lowland men of the capital would find it easy to dismiss the ghost story as Highland superstition especially as the two witnesses themselves were not in total agreement. The trial came to an end on 12 June with the defendants being acquitted, the reason supposedly being that the jurors were offended by the idea of ghostly testimony, even as hearsay. They also perhaps thought Alexander MacPherson himself had something to hide. The acquittal of the accused suggests that even citizens of Edinburgh had had enough of the behaviour of the Redcoats in Scotland and had decided that enough Highlanders had been hanged, innocent or not! Ironically, local tradition never has had any doubt as to the guilt of the two men accused!

A curse on Little Alan

⇒◆⇐

Despite over a millennium of the religion, the Highlanders of Scotland held on to many beliefs that sat ill with Christianity. The well known, if rare, gift – though often considered more of a curse by those who had it – of second-sight ensured a healthy level of respect for prophecy, even amongst regular church-goers. There was also a widely held belief in the powers of wise-women, people of considerable knowledge and abilities, whom the priests always saw as little more than witches. In the '15, a chieftain on the island of South Uist, Alan Beag MacDonald, was setting off with the rest of the men of the Clan Ranald when one of these women put a charm on him to protect him from all harm. Such charms were believed to be very effective. When MacLeod of Berneray returned home from Culloden thirty years later without a scratch, his kinfolk attributed it to a similar charm. Now, Alan Beag was of course rounding up as many of his clansmen as he could, and he picked a young lad from a clachan at Stoneybridge, near Ormacleit, to go along with the rest. His mother was a widow and the young lad, her only son.

'Please, please don't take my young lad. He is only fifteen and he is all I have,' she pleaded, but her pleas fell on deaf ears.

'I myself was in battle at his age, and his clan has need of him at this time,' was the reply she got.

Now, she knew of the spell that had been put on Allan, but she too was a woman of knowledge and decided to have her own revenge on the chieftain for his insistence on taking her son, which she saw as unjust. So she cursed Alan Beag that he would never see his home again. But it would be as well to mak siccar, she thought to herself.

Before her son left to join the Earl of Mar with the mustered men of the clan she baked two bannocks, the standard unleavened barley or oat bread of the Highlands. One was small and the other very big indeed.

She put them both on the table and said to her son, 'Now, you must choose which to take. You can have the big one with my curse or the little one with my blessing.'

The lad, no fool, replied, 'I would rather have the little one with your blessing mother.'

So she gave him the little bannock and put her hand in the pouch at the front of her apron and drew out a bent, silver sixpence coin.

'Here, my son, is a crooked sixpence which has been seven times cursed!' she said, and she went on to tell him what he must do for her or else fall under her curse.

Weeks later, the MacDonald contingent were to the fore in the battle with the Hanoverians at Sheriffmuir and the musket balls were whistling all around Alan Beag like midgies. Not one touched him as he cut the enemy down like thistles. The battle at this point was totally in the balance with any advantage the Highlanders had in one spot being offset by their being on the defensive in another part of the fighting. The young lad had fallen a little behind the line of battle, having acquitted himself well at the start of fighting, and, as he caught his breath, he heard his mother's voice, as clear as if she was standing beside him, speaking over all of the hellish noise of battle with gunshots, war-cries and the shriek of the dead and dying. 'Let it avail ye in battle against Alan Beag and so take my blessing for if you do otherwise my curse shall be upon you.'

As if in a trance, he took the crooked sixpence from his sporran and loaded it into the musket he had been given and trained to use. He raised it and pointed it to where his chieftain was thrusting his basket-hilted sword into the body of a red-coated soldier. Through the swirling smoke he took aim. He fired. At once Alan fell dead. As the word spread that their chieftain had fallen, a great cry went up from the Clanranald men, and they started to keen and moan. No one had seen the young lad fire; they had all been concentrating on their enemy to the front.

Glengarry, leading his own contingent of MacDonalds to their left, saw what was happening. At once, he left his position with his own kin and ran amongst the Uist men, waving his bonnet to catch their attention and crying above the noise of the battle, 'Today for revenge, tomorrow for weeping.'

The Clanranald men fell on the Hanoverians like berserkers of old in their fury, and there are those who will say that this is why the right wing of the Jacobite army forced the troops before them to turn and flee. After the battle, with great sorrow and a lone piper preceding them playing a coronach, the South Uist Clanranalds lifted the body of their fallen chief and took it to Drummond Castle, near Muthill a few miles to the north. Here, they laid the body of their chieftain to rest, far from the land of his kin.

Back in South Uist at Ormacleit a strange thing happened that same night. Ever since her husband had left, Allan's wife had had a premonition that something bad was about to happen to the new house they lived in. This had been built by French masons with the best of imported materials and had taken all of seven years to build. Nothing like it had been seen in the Uists, or many of the islands before. It was exactly seven years since they inhabited the house that the Battle of Sherrifmuir took place and the leader of

Clanranald fell. The life had not long left his body when that very same night the new house at Ormacleit caught fire and was burned to the ground. It was a sad loss but nothing like the loss of Alan Beag MacDonald to his kinfolk.

The Appin Dirk

⬅◆➡

In June 1746 a bunch of Redcoats were looting their way through Appin, along the shores of Loch Linnhe on the way to Inverary. One evening, as they were marching along the north shore of Loch Laich, they noticed a young woman in a nearby field adjoining the loch milking a cow. With a laugh, the sergeant in charge of the company leapt over the dyke, raised his musket and shot the cow dead. This was greeted with laughter by his fellows, who thought this a great joke.

'Well done, Sarge,' came a cry. 'That Highland bitch looks young and healthy; why don't you give her a go?'

This suggestion was met with shouts of agreement from the rest of the men, and the sergeant turned to look at them with a big smile. He put down his gun, took off his hat and placed it on the ground. Then he turned and started making his way towards the young lass, unfastening his jacket as he did so, his intention quite obvious. Catriona McColl, though she had no word of English, realised what the soldier had in mind, especially as she saw others climbing the dyke into the field and putting down their weapons. She was a strong-willed and capable lass and had heard the stories of these foul southron soldiers raping women all over the Highlands. There was no way she was going to meekly submit to this foul creature. She bent down and picked up a fist-sized stone. This made the sergeant laugh as he threw off his jacket, and he began to run at her. Back went her arm. Straight flew the stone, striking the sergeant on the temple and knocking him to the ground, where he lay supine. The rest of the soldiers gasped at this, and, as they ran to their fallen companion, Catriona took the opportunity to sprint to the lochside, where she knew there was a boat tied up. Since her infancy she had been used to handling boats, and it was a matter of seconds for her to push it off and start rowing out into the loch.

By the time some of the soldiers ran down to the shore, she had gone a good way off. The soldiers had to run back to where they had dropped their weapons, just a minute or two earlier, with something other than shooting on their minds. By the time some of them had got back to the shore with their weapons loaded and cocked she had put a fair distance between herself and the shore, and the shots they fired after her were well wide of the mark. Once Catriona was sure she was well out of range she relaxed a bit and looked back to see the soldiers lift their fallen comrade and carry him back to the road. She then carried on rowing, heading out of Loch Laich and eventually landing on one of the small islands off the north coast of Lismore. The boat belonged to her cousin Lachlan, and, in the circumstances, she was sure he wouldn't mind if he didn't have the use of it for a day or so. She hauled the boat up out of the water and into the scrub on the island. Then, she sat down to wait. Luckily, the weather stayed calm, and, once it was dark, she rowed back to the mainland, using the lights from Portnacrosh as a guide. On landing, she hurried home, sure that no one would tell the soldiers who she was. If she kept out of sight for the next few days things would probably blow over.

After her escape the soldiers were furious and carried their wounded sergeant to a house in the nearby clachan of Tynribbie, which they took over, driving out the inhabitants with blows and curses. However, despite their attentions, by the morning the sergeant had died from the blow to his head. They were under orders to proceed as quickly as they could to Inverary and, although they wanted to have their revenge on the local populace, they were already behind schedule. The corporal now in charge thought it best to head off after burying the body in the kirkyard at Kinlochlaich. As they left they swore at the local populace and promised they would back to find the bitch who had murdered their sergeant.

Word of what had happened had spread quickly round the area and, as soon as the party of soldiers had left the area, a group of men arrived at the sergeant's grave. They had no intention of letting his body lie in this holy ground amongst their ancestors, so they dug the body up and dragged it down to the seashore, where they threw it into the water to let the tide deal with it. However, on the way to the shore Catriona's brother, Donald, took the opportunity to remove the skin from one of the forearms of the corpse. He then cured and treated the skin before making a sheath for his dirk from it. A grisly heirloom indeed, which was passed down in his family for many generations and was locally called the Appin Dirk.

A show trial

In the aftermath of the '45 many estates were forfeited to the crown. Historians have presented this as, effectively, the seizure of the property of great landowners. However, although many of the chiefs were well on the way to rationalising the communal lands of the entire clan into their own personal property – a change much sought after by the Government as it removed the ties that bound the clan chiefs to their warriors – the situation was not clear cut. Many clansfolk were now paying rent, but the Highland economy was still in many ways based on self-sufficiency and rents had traditionally been paid in kind. This had allowed the chiefs to hold considerable stores of grain and other goods, which were often needed in the subsistence economy of the Highlands when, for instance, crops failed due to bad weather. It was also the chief's duty to look after those who could not look after themselves, like the old and the infirm. Such duties had always been part of the clan chief's role for he was never a feudal overlord; he was the centre of a complex and dynamic system of kinship relations, and his place at the head of the society was simply by virtue of the fact that he was the closest to the original founder of the clan, from whom all took their name.

The policy of building the Wade Roads from 1726 onwards had always had an additional role on top of their primary function of allowing quick troop movement to control the Highland warrior clans. This role was to open up the Highlands to the money economy of the rest of the island of Britain and to erode the ancient, self-sufficient, kin-based systems that underpinned the clans. Although the chiefs by now had legal ownership of the clan lands, it was the ancient kinship system underpinning Highland society that allowed them to bring their clansmen from the glens and straths to fight in the Jacobite army.

Even when the Government did take over the so-called estates, really clan territories, after the '45, exacting what rents they could, this did not break the ties between the people on those lands and their chiefs, many of whom had fled abroad. The loyalty of the people was to the clan, and the clan was represented in the chief himself. In fact, in some instances, clanspeople were sending second rents abroad to their exiled chiefs, a practice which helped keep the Highlands in dire poverty for a considerable time. Of course, when running these 'estates', the Government had to choose people who they considered loyal and efficient. In many cases this meant Campbells, a clan who had long seen the value of the money economy and had a history of stealing land from other, less powerful, clans. In terms of the modern British money-based economy they understood what needed to be done. Forward-thinking, efficient and usually hardworking by their own lights, they were seen as little more than traitors by many other clans. Their espousal of the Hanoverian cause was considered by many as just another instance of their essential venality and greed. What cannot be doubted is that they had a great talent for seeing which way the wind was blowing!

One of the Campbells chosen to factor a forfeited estate was Colin Campbell of Glenure, a man known as the Red Fox. It was typical of Government actions of the time that in 1746, after banning any Highlander from acting as the factor for any Highland estate, they imposed Campbell as factor on the estates of Ardhseal, Callart and Mamore, in Appin. This was the country of the Stewarts, the closest of all the clans to the exiled dynasty. Part of Government policy was to evict all those it considered a possible future threat, so James Stewart of Glenduror was evicted on Whitsunday 1751 and his lands handed over to Campbell of Ballievolan. Now, Stewart was a well-respected man known as James of the Glens for his skills as a hunter and mountaineer. A lifelong Jacobite, he had been an officer in the '45, and he took the eviction hard. The Red Fox had the army behind him and James knew there was little he could do. Still, he was heart-broken that he had been evicted from the land of his forefathers, and one night, slightly the worse for wear in a local hostelry, he was heard to say, 'Curse that man. I would go three miles on my hands and knees to put an end to him.' He was among friends, but in those troubled times the Government had spies everywhere, and his words were soon passed on to the Red Fox.

The following year, 14 May, the Red Fox set out from Fort William to carry on the policy he had been implementing with vigour over the previous months – evicting Stewart families from their ancestral homes. He was accompanied by his nephew, Mungo Campbell, the sheriff's officer from Inverary; a servant of sorts called Mackenzie and a party of mounted dragoons. Glenure well knew that he was hated by the people of the area and had had word that some Camerons were set to attack him and his party. Some say that he and his companions were unarmed, but in those times, when there were still bands of Jacobite caterans roaming the Scottish Highlands, this would have been foolish indeed. As it was, however, he managed to escape an ambush that had been set up for him by some of the Camerons and passed through Lochaber. His party reached the ferry at Ballachulish in safety and crossed over to the south side of Loch Leven without incident. They then proceeded to ride south along the shores of Loch Linnhe towards Kentallen. They were riding along not far from the ferry on the slopes of *Leitir Mhor* when there was the sound of gunfire from somewhere behind and above them. The Red Fox slumped forward and, raising himself as his horse reared up, called out, 'Oh, I am dead,' and fell from his horse to the ground. At once, his nephew dismounted to see to him while the soldiers turned and looked up to where the shots had come from to see a figure disappearing into the woods. Mackenzie was sent for help and the soldiers headed off after the gunman while Mungo and Finlayson, the sheriff's officer, stayed with Glenure. There was nothing they could do. Two bullets had pierced his spine and come through the front of his chest. He died as he lay there by the road. The soldiers were soon back. They could find no sign to follow in the thick underbrush of the woods and could see little point looking further.

The story of Glenure's death, which most of the local population thought justice rather than murder, was soon being passed from clachan to clachan and glen to glen all through Appin and Lochaber. James of the Glens was working in his fields when he heard the news. He stopped, the blood drained from his face and he uttered the words, 'Whoever has done this, I shall pay, mark my words,' then went on sowing oats.

The immediate suspect was Allan Breck Stewart, a professional soldier who had served in the British Army before deserting to join the Jacobite army in 1745. He was a prime target for the Government troops and was known to have been in the area. In truth, it could have been any one of a hundred men, but the Campbells needed a scapegoat. Allan Breck, if it was him, had gone to ground, but the Government knew where James of the Glens was. He had also recently been to the Court of Session in Edinburgh to try and put a stop to the evictions of his kin by Glenure. Within days a troop of horsemen rode into Glen Duror and arrested James for complicity in the murder of Campbell of

Glenure. He was taken off to Inverary, the heart of the Campbells' lands. Whoever it was that killed Glenure – and the people of Appin kept it secret a long time – it was known, without doubt, that it was not James Stewart of Glen Duror. He even had witnesses to where he was at the time of the fatal shooting but, when the time came, they were not called to give evidence. Revenge and the squashing of potential future resistance were the watchwords of the court that eventually sat; it was said that Justice was a stranger in that court and there can be little doubt of it.

The judges were the Duke of Argyll, Scotland's Lord Justice General, chief of the Clan Campbell and a close relative of the deceased; Sir James Fergusson; Lord Kilkerran; and Patrick Grant, Lord Elchies, who had a reputation as a hanging judge. Both of the latter owed their positions as judges to the patronage of the Duke of Argyll. Of the fifteen men that these learned judges chose to try James Stewart, eleven were Campbells. When the charge was laid it was not murder but merely that he had been an accessory to Allan Breck Stewart in the murder of Colin Campbell of Glenure. The fact that Allan Breck had never been caught, tried and found guilty, or even charged with the crime was irrelevant. They had the opportunity to rid themselves of James Stewart and they took it. After all, somebody had to pay for the crime and it might as well be a man they considered a thorn in their flesh, a man around whom resistance to their oppression of the people of Lochaber and Appin might well form. There was not even an attempt to pretend that justice was being done.

In his summing up, the Lord Chief Justice of Scotland, the country's leading law official, had these words to say to an innocent man: 'If you had been successful in that rebellion, you had now been triumphant with your confederates, trampling upon the laws of your country, the liberties of your fellow subjects

262

and on the Protestant religion. You might have been giving the law where you have now received the judgement of it; and we, who are this day your judges, might have been tried before one of your mock courts of judicature, and then you might have been satiated with the blood of any name or clan to which you had an aversion, though you do not now stand accused as a rebel, yet this murder has been visibly the effect and consequence of the late rebellion.' Argyll could hardly have described his own behaviour better.

The sentence, like the verdict, was a foregone conclusion. It is said that at the time some of the more boastful Campbells were heard saying, 'Ach, it's nothing to have a guilty man hanged, but only MacCailein Mor [the Duke of Argyll] can hang an innocent man when he likes!'

And so James was hanged, with all the world knowing he was innocent of the crime he had been charged with. Under an escort of a hundred soldiers, he was taken to a spot near the present Ballachulish Hotel, and there he ascended the gallows. He protested his innocence of the charge and declared his continued adherence to the Episcopalian faith and the Jacobite cause before he was finally hanged. His body was left swinging in the wind, with a guard of soldiers to make sure no one came and took away the corpse for burial. After several months the skeleton fell apart, but the Government and their Campbell allies were not satisfied. A soldier was instructed to attach the bones of the skeleton back together with wire and re-hang the bones! The symbol of Government control and Campbell power had to remain to remind people who was now in charge! It was the following year before a wandering madman was induced to cut down the bones and throw the gibbet into Loch Linnhe. The skeleton was recovered at Bunawe and buried, secretly, at night, in Keil churchyard in Duror. For years the locals would take people to the site of the gallows and show them the holes where the poles for the gibbet had been, telling them that even the very earth was so offended at the treatment of James of the Glens that it refused to close up. As for Allan Breck, well, he made it safely to the Continent to resume his life as a professional soldier. He never saw Scotland again, dying many years later in Paris. On the day James of the Glens was hanged the man who did fire the fatal shot had to be tied down by his relatives to prevent him coming to the gibbet to proclaim his own guilt and James's innocence. He was racked with guilt, but his relations knew fine that nothing would deflect the fate the Campbells had decreed for James of the Glens; it would be a pointless sacrifice to give himself up.

Although many people still refer to the incident as the Appin murder, the locals at the time thought that the Red Fox got no more than he deserved, and it has been said round the hearths of many Appin homes that there had been a shooting contest days before the event, the prize, the privilege of shooting Colin Campbell of Glenure.

Down the centuries since this event there has been much speculation about the assailant, but the people of Appin kept their secret, though in recent years there has been strong confirmation that the man who won the shooting match, Donald Stewart of Ballachulish, was, in fact, the man who killed the Red Fox.